D0426603

Also by Stephanie Brush:
MEN: AN OWNER'S MANUAL

Stephanie Brush

THE LINDEN PRESS/SIMON AND SCHUSTER

NEW YORK 1987

Published by The Linden Press/Simon and Schuster
A Division of Simon & Schuster, Inc.
Simon & Schuster Building
Rockefeller Center
1230 Avenue of the Americas
New York, New York 10020
THE LINDEN PRESS/SIMON AND SCHUSTER and colophon are
trademarks of Simon & Schuster, Inc.
Designed by Karolina Harris
Manufactured in the United States of America

10 9 8 7 6 5 4 3 2 1

Library of Congress Cataloging-in-Publication Data
Brush, Stephanie.
Life, a warning.

I. Title.
PN6162.B78 1987 818′.5402 86-27501
ISBN: 0-671-61130-5

for you, Bob

Contents

There is a story about a mountain climber who was nearly freezing to death in the Swiss Alps when, miraculously, he found a little door in the sheer, vertical face of the rock, in the middle of nowhere—and he tried it, and it opened to his touch, *and he crawled inside where it was warm and dry, and he lay in exhaustion, until he saw a strange light right in front of him that grew larger and sharper and brighter.*

And he realized he had wandered into a railroad tunnel in the side of the mountain, and was now lying directly in the path of an oncoming train.

This story is being told not so much to put a crimp in your day as to remind you that the climber did *roll out of the way in time, or how else do you imagine he would have lived to tell about it?*

"Life" will always be highly dangerous for its participants, but it will always be much more popular than its obvious alternative.

Even if the light at the end of the tunnel is the 12:52 to Geneva and Chamonix, if you escape with only minor injuries, you should think rather carefully before you start complaining.

That's Life, and this is just a friendly warning.

I

Life: the Basics

We Are the World; We Are the Fretful

ALL of us are brought into the world with the same basic operating parts. All, if not most, of us are given bodies, and some, if not all, of us are given brains.

What happens to the human body in the course of one's lifetime is no mystery. Eventually, all of us must succumb to the rigors of old age, the crucible of athlete's foot, the time-trials of puberty, the itching and flare-up of painful hemorrhoidal tissue—in one order or another.

While our bodies are in the process of waging a constant, fairly messy skirmish against Time, our minds are up against only one thing (but it's kind of a big one): Life Itself.

If we had been born with bodies but no brains (an experiment which has been tried with reasonable success in much of Southern California), we could avoid so many of the worst uncertainties Life has to offer.

BUT OUR BRAINS NEVER REST.

If there is one simple factor that unifies all of mankind, it is probably that everyone is afraid of something. Paradoxically, we seem to fear both death and living at the same time. And if you say, "Oh, pshaw" to this, when was the last time you leaped out of bed with a conquering smile, a passionate heart, and a boundless love for all humanity? *Few people are not innately suspicious of "getting up in the morning."*

It is like the "trauma of birth" all over again. Even if you never read a lot of Kafka and are free of the fear of waking up as a giant cockroach, you probably did watch *The Twilight Zone* as a child, and know that any number of things can happen that you have no way of predicting.

YOU NEVER KNOW IF YOU WILL WAKE UP:

- In a parallel universe
- In a movie version of your own life
- As a robot version of yourself
- Eight inches tall
- In a world where everyone looks like actor SHELLEY BERMAN. (There was an actual episode where this happened. LOOK IT UP.)

DEFINING ESSENTIAL TERMS

A lot of people are confused about the difference between a "fear" and a "phobia." It is an important distinction.

A "fear" is something that you are personally taking the time and valuable effort to be afraid of. A "phobia" is something only crazy people are afraid of. Let's say, for example, you are afraid of being bitten by rabid beavers on a camping trip and you try to never venture into woodsy areas where there are rustlings and little munchy noises in the foliage. That is a fear. Someone *else's* fear of rabid beavers is a phobia.

Nowadays there are so many terrible things happening on the 6 O'Clock News, our minds are cooking up unprecedented orchestrations of fears and phobias, which are often virtually paralyzing to our modern way of life. What we have failed to do, of course, is see the whole matter in perspective.

A SHORT HISTORY OF PARALYZING FEAR

In point of fact, we're just on our way out of living in probably the *safest* century in human history. All the wars were going on in certifiably "unsafe" hemispheres where we didn't have to look at them, everyone called the postman "Larry," and Wally and Beaver Cleaver could safely ride the train to Mayfield (even though they'd spent all their fare money on comic books) because they knew the kindly train conductor would give them money out of his own pocket. There were no sex perverts. There was no radon gas. Nobody ever had to save the whales because the whales were all pretty much okay.

BUT FOR ABOUT FIVE THOUSAND YEARS OF HUMAN HISTORY, NONE OF THIS WAS TRUE AT ALL.

You had various Ice Ages that lasted about a thousand years apiece, okay? Then you had the Fall of Rome, the Dark Ages, the Diet of Worms, the Black Death, and a number of other events which left people constantly fearful, insecure, and completely exhausted. You had press-gangs and hussars and buccaneers wandering around in almost constant supply, pillaging most things that were not nailed down.

For about two thousand years in Europe, you had Thundering Hordes abounding. If you lived in the Countryside, you had Genghis Khan, or other Filthy Barbarians, knocking at your gate and dragging your daughters off to their tents. (All of the Thundering Hordes had little color maps of Europe, and they were following little gray arrows which told them whether to Thunder north, south, east, or inland —and all the while the Abject Peasants were shrieking for succor; they knew they would have to sweep up all the rubbish left in the wake of the Hordes, and then go home and die of consumption.) No one ever said, *Time Out. I don't want to live this way anymore.*

AND HERE WE ARE *COMPLAINING* because we have enough strategic weapons to destroy all of human life a hundred times.

Clearly, modern fear is not all that big a deal.

And yet modern fear does have a unique *character*—a *body* —a *clarity* all its own. We invented it; we fermented it; and we're now just kind of stuck with a *soft* spot for it. . . .

THE BIG FIVE POPULAR FEARS OF OUR TIME

In a recent survey, 1,000 Americans were asked to name the fear that torments them the most. They're listed here in no particular order-of-fearsomeness, but most everyone has a personal favorite on this list.

1. Fear of Gradual Hysteria

Gradual hysteria is what happens when you feel your life is completely out of control.

Many of us attempt to exert control by redecorating our homes, for example. We move a picture and find that there is a rectangular spot on the wall where the picture used to be. Then we move the TV stand and find that there are four identical indentations in the rug. Then we move the TV stand back and find that there are now eight identical indentations in the rug. Then someone starts drilling into the pavement outside the window, and the phone rings exactly once, and stops, and we run to answer it, and hear only a metallic click and start to scream, very quietly. We feel that God is talking to us. "Just try it," He is saying. "Just try and make something out of your life."

Gradual hysteria happens in this way to just about everybody. It is usually triggered by loud noises, helplessness, and cumulative stress, and yes, it has the power to destroy everything in its path. But you'd rather have that happening to you than to someone else, wouldn't you?

2. Fear of People Who Have Had Too Much Assertiveness Training

There was a movement back in the seventies in which thousands of ineffectual nebbishes decided that they were not standing firm where it counted in life, and they went out and shelled out $300 at adult-education classes around the country, so that they could Learn to Say No! To Get Their Needs Met! To Not Take a Lot of BS From the Guy at the Auto Body Shop!

They walk among us now, and the threat they pose is inestimable.

Have they become, in fact, "assertive" people? Let's be serious. Assertiveness comes from being *born* knowing you're going to get the goods in life, whatever they may be. You don't have to take *courses* in this stuff, okay? And the reason an assertiveness-trained nebbish is a dangerous commodity is that he suspects he is still a nebbish but he's not sure whether it shows or not. *It shows,* all right?

He starts to breathe heavily at the cleaners' because he's just found a spot on his jacket that wasn't there before, and now he is trying to remember his "lines" for the big confrontation to come.

Sometimes, Assertiveness-Trained Nebbishes get the heady feeling of "being honest" and "owning their feelings"—and they do embarrassing things like embrace you and say, "I hate your rug, but the honesty of this moment feels beautiful."

Whatever we do, it is essential for us to impress on our friends that we liked them better when they were obsequious, waffling little toadies. At least then we knew what we were dealing with. At least life had some kind of structure.

There is some work being done to "de-program" these people, sort of like former members of cults. But it is too soon to tell whether this technique is going to have any effect.

3.
Insomnia: Fear of Consciousness

"Consciousness" is a state of awareness of all the realities of life. If we had to live in a state of total awareness all the time, if we had to dwell on realities like crime and war and what happens to the members of "Menudo" after they turn fifteen, then we should all surely become mad and highly depressed.

So sleep was invented to spare us from total consciousness. But the more we can't sleep, the more conscious—and therefore *anxious*—we become. The same scientists who have clocked things like REM cycles and muscle-activity cycles have also clocked pre-sleep anxiety cycles.

- Cycle I usually involves WORK ANXIETY: Did I remember to turn off my office light? Does my boss like me? Would my boss recognize me if he saw me in a small crowd?
- Cycle II involves CURRENT-EVENTS ANXIETY: Is there plutonium in my drinking water? Will the world be safe for my children? With street crime in the state it's in, would it be all right if I asked my dog to walk himself at night?
- Cycle III occurs when the mind drifts off to a netherworld of half-formed dreads and sinister potentialities. What if my family got sick and died? What if they were tied to a stake in the Amazon rain forest and eaten by termites? What if I were on a quiz show and had to know the Gross National Product of Burma?

Some of these fears, unfortunately, have more than a little merit (although for what it's worth, the GNP of Burma is 657,000 Bwenzii a year, and there are no termites in the Amazon rain forest. Then again, there's nothing to stop them from being flown in.)

It is estimated that over 45 percent of the population suffers from insomnia on any given night; which means that on any given night YOU ARE ALONE WITH 150 MILLION OTHER AMERICANS. So when you think about it, it would make sense if you were given these people's phone numbers, so you'd at least have someone to talk to. (And yet, paradoxically, if you called them, they would scream into the receiver, "What are you, *crazy*? It's *three o'clock in the morning*!" And they would call the police.)

4.
Fear of Amnesia

There are really three varieties of amnesia we need to talk about here:

"Random" amnesia strikes about 5 million Americans a year, including an undisclosed number of dental patients who "forget" to floss between meals, and a number of hotel guests who "forget" to return the towels, stationery, and light fixtures to the rooms where they found them. Also every year, twelve or thirteen natives of Florence, Oregon, fall victim to *group* amnesia and awaken and imagine themselves to be natives of Florence, Italy. They immediately start painting frescoes all over the sides of municipal buildings, and each year the frescoes have to be sandblasted off, at the expense of thousands to the taxpayers, since no one in Oregon is known to have any artistic talent.

By far the most virulent form of amnesia is SOAPSTAR amnesia, which occurs relentlessly in daytime television. Hardly a day goes by when someone on one of the major networks is not suffering from a complete memory loss—*"What do you mean 'Nicki Matuszak?' I've never heard of a 'Nicki Matuszak' in my life! I'm a beekeeper! Stay away from me!"*

These poor doomed sufferers are destined to wander around strange towns in brunette wigs and unattractive clothing, marry people they have never met before, and ignore the pleas of their husbands and wives on television ("Nicki! It's me, Stefano! I never meant to shoot you in the brain! Please come home!").

Naturally, if we watch a lot of daytime TV, we are afraid that this fate could befall us (although we secretly wonder how TV amnesiacs can use their American Express cards for months at a time, pay the finance charge, and still not have a clue to their identity).

5.
Fear of Major Brain-Loss

Many people are afraid of appearing helpless, foolish, and "brainless." For example, of being in serious car crashes and becoming "vegetables." (Although if you get incinerated in a *plane* crash, you get to become a "mineral," which is probably much, much worse.)

A far greater threat than this, however, is that of having a song you really hate running through your head that you just can't get rid of. It certainly happens more frequently. NO ONE EVER HAS A SONG THEY *LIKE* RUNNING THROUGH THEIR HEAD. Large numbers of college graduates still hear "Yummy, Yummy, Yummy," by the Ohio Express, and some people have gone nearly insane with a continual rendition of "Hey! You! Get Offa My Cloud!" as performed by the Ray Conniff Singers.

Add to the dangers of brain-loss the persistent lure of religious cults, lurking tantalizingly with "all the answers" around every corner. Beyond even the Hare Krishnas and the Unification Church lies the "Pepsi Generation," a dangerous cult headed by singer LIONEL RICHIE. Instead of working regular hours and contributing to the Gross National Product, the Pepsi Generation spends hours taking dancing lessons and having their teeth professionally polished. They venerate organized volleyball and drive dune buggies to all their major appointments. Fortunately, they are closely watched and monitored by a number of federal agencies.

A BIG CONCERN

As terrible as the fear of existence is, the fear of nonexistence is even worse. Maybe if we only knew what happened to us after we died, it would all be easier.

One speculation is that we go to the Land of the Umbrellas. You've probably seen them at the end of every rainstorm. Lying in the gutter, crumpled, skeletal, inside-out, bereft of personal history. Who did these umbrellas belong to? Where are they going? What use are they now?

Others say that after death we go to the land of the M&M's—the place where the M&M's go after they fall behind the cushions on the sofa. Or some say it's the land of the Other Shoe. (Ever drive along the road and see one shoe lying on the pavement, and wonder how it got there? You never see *both shoes*; the other shoe has gone to join the umbrellas and the M&M's.)

In the end it is probably foolish to speculate about such matters. In ancient times the biggest fear was that you would have a terrible life and be reincarnated, and the next life would be even worse. Nowadays, life is Hollywood, and if your life's been bad, you don't have to worry about there being a sequel. Not if Part I didn't make any money.

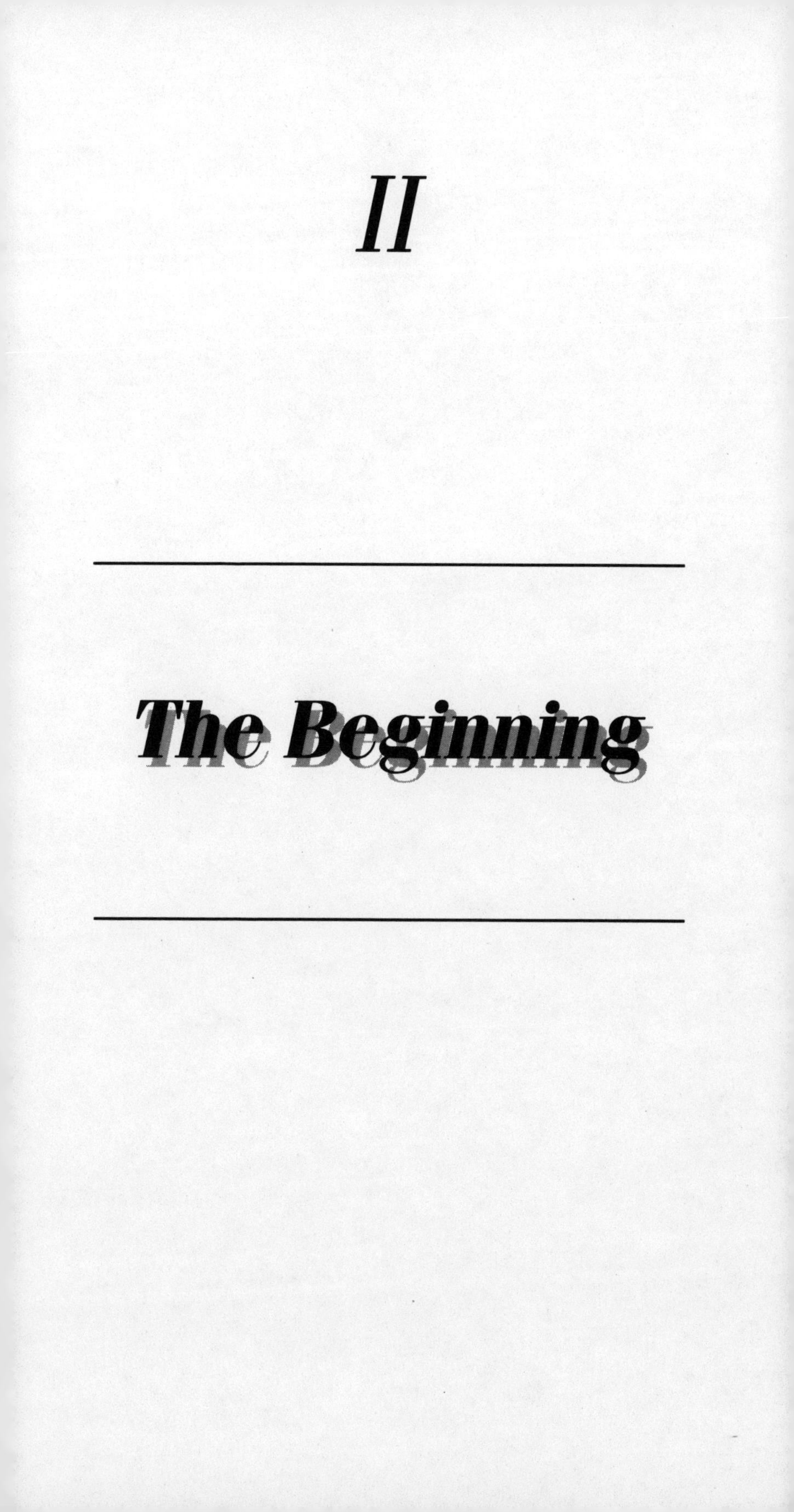

II

The Beginning

Your Major Ingredients

THERE are two schools of thought about human development. One states that growth is a series of well-defined steps with discrete transitions in between, while the other claims that growth is a "continuum." For example, in a "typical" growth pattern, a boy might learn to play with small, furry animals, grow up, attend college, and then become the chairman of the board of a large, rapacious Wall Street investment firm. In that order.

It is not likely that he will become the chairman of the board of Dean Witter Reynolds and *then* ask his parents for a puppy named Sparky. Certain elements of the structure of life are inviolable, no matter how we may wish to change them.

BIRTH ORDER

Many experts feel that your destiny is truly shaped according to whether you're an "older," a "younger," or a "middle." Either you are the bright, shining Prince of the Universe (the first son) or you are Gordon Padilla's snotty little brother.

Everyone seemingly wants to be the "oldest" (or "Khan," or "God"; whatever) because you always get the newest clothes, and more Polaroids taken of you with a succession of cakes on your face, and so on. The idyll is almost always shattered by the birth of additional beings in the house. It seems to happen even in the best of families. The inevitable, scalding realization that NO ONE ON EARTH EVER GETS ALL THE OREOS TO HIMSELF. (Only Muammar Khaddafi has tried to challenge this truism in recent years, with varying results.)

All older children feel that they are "not good enough" when a younger sibling is born. Not, somehow, "up to snuff." They come to feel that somehow they were born a "Ford Pinto," and are in effect being "recalled by the manufacturer." Maybe you tried to look closely at the face of your sister at birth, and it looked like a stewed grape, and you thought "*This* is an improvement?" This is why it is normal to hate your brother Larry well into adulthood, because you are convinced that long after graduation, when he got his job at the greeting-card store, your mother was still breast-feeding him, and lying about it to your father.

Delicious stories about the terrorization of younger siblings fill the record books. A boy in Grand Island, Nebraska, once kept his three sisters locked in a tornado cellar until they could correctly recite all the state capitals (they all failed on "Olympia, Washington"—most people do) and one of them received so little oxygen during her incarceration that she was slightly brain-damaged for the rest of her life. (In her sleep she used to yell, "Oklahoma City! Tallahassee! Baton Rouge—*no, Little Rock*!" until someone had to stuff a rag in her mouth.) She later became a professional guest on quiz shows.

PROBABLY THE BIGGEST FACTOR

Very early in childhood, by age three at the latest, you notice a compelling sexual dichotomy in life that will haunt you until the day you die. That there is an incontrovertible "difference" between boys and girls: boys get black ice skates for Christmas, and girls get white ones. This is an unchanging, eternal truth, and with it comes the knowledge that you will never see Gordy Howe skimming across the ice in a white tutu, performing selections from *Swan Lake,* in the beam of a powder blue spotlight. Most girls know by the age of five that they will never be centers for the New York Rangers, and they learn to endure the knowledge and still lead full, productive lives.

Female children have a whole range of troubling questions to ask their mothers: Why are the presidents and joint chiefs of staff always men? Why, for years, was there a Mr. Potato Head, and why was *Mrs.* Potato Head treated like a virtual afterthought? Why are there no female game-show hosts?

This is why mothers play such an important role in a child's early development. By answering the most perplexing questions of the universe ("How do people in tollbooths go to the bathroom?" uppermost among them), Mom's voice becomes assimilated into the brain of the child, is assigned a series of cerebral call letters, and becomes, in effect, "Radio Mom."

It was over This Same Station, however, that you were issued the "regulations" that you were least inclined to want to live with on a regular basis.

It was a rule of thumb, for example, that your mother never wanted you to play with the kids that were the best kids to play with. There was always one kid in particular that whenever your mother heard his name, she made a face like she just smelled burning human fingernails, and you could never figure out why.

This is because the best kids to play with were usually the ones that *lied* the most.

Kids who lied were usually the most popular, for reasons of evolution. Lying was a standard, survival-linked trait, going back to the Stone Age. Early civilization always had a shining member of the community who told great stories, and bright as a button during a famine, could say, "Listen, I saw a whole *ton* of food down by the tar pits," and when everyone had gone running barefoot with all the receptacles they could find, this fine gentleman would eat up all their shoes.

THE ETERNAL MORAL CRISIS

Almost from birth, a child's parents instill in him a "moral code"—a sense of shame in doing wrong, and saintly gladness in doing right. And yet the child sees his mother taking eleven items into the Express Line at the supermarket and he sees his father buying rec-room lighting fixtures shaped like golf tees and declaring them to the IRS as a business expense, and he sees his sister applying bogus cosmetic facial contours to a face that is in fact boneless, before a date. He says, "So, that's the game, eh?"

Everywhere he looks, the child sees adults sucking up to people whom they cannot possibly like personally and suffering no ill effects whatever from the practice. (This is known as "good business." A child's first experience with calculated, conniving, and blatant flattery is usually traumatic, because he is horrified to see how effectively it works. As long as he's a child it never works on *him,* but he's afraid that when he's an adult, it might. And he is right—it will.)

A child is told things like "Virtue is *its own reward,*" but he feels that "a system of cash rebates" would be much more effective, based on what he's seen of the world.

This is why children start to toy with the moral machinery of life at an early age. To see if they can find a crack they can widen and work with.

AN EARLY BRUSH WITH THE HEREAFTER

Somewhere along the line, most children will ask for, and receive, a live animal, usually a hamster, for Christmas. Craving a hamster is a unique form of child/parent extortion, because for the first nine years of your life, your parents will have a number of very sound reasons for not giving you a hamster.

Then, when you are about eleven, they will run dry of excuses, and the night before Christmas you will hear scratching noises in the closet, and your mother will say, "Oh, that must be the *elves,* Jimmy," and you will say, "Save it, Mom. *Elves*?" You think that your loss of innocence is a time of sadness for your parents, but they don't really waste their time feeling wistful so much as they just sort of hate you for several weeks. There are now a lot fewer things they can lie to you about, and they know that somehow, in some way, this is going to come out of their wallets.

Most pet stores will give your parents a "guarantee" on the life span of a hamster. It runs along the lines of seven days. (At Christmastime your parents are used to having outrageous figures and numbers quoted at them, so "seven days" will fall into that kind of macabre netherworld of "Right now I'll believe anything. Why don't you just shoot me?")

Parents mostly realize that hamsters fall into the realm of "metaphorical" pets. For their six-day life span they run like blazes on a little plastic wheel in pursuit of a little hamster "grail" of some kind that they cannot consciously identify, and then they drop dead of some arbitrary hamster ailment when the clock strikes twelve, and you feel a Squeeze from the Hand of Eternity that you never imagined before.

"Where has Squeaky gone to?" you ask your mother, and she tells you that there are treadmills in Heaven. (In fact, the Power Company in Heaven is run by a sort of Hamster Mafia, and thousands of ghostly hamsters are up there pedaling away, and they will do that for all eternity.)

This experience is a major watershed in the life of a child, and the sign of a major shift in values.

HOW MUCH DO *MOM AND DAD KNOW?*

It is true that before becoming parents at all, most parents have to sign a written statement *swearing* that they will always give three pieces of advice to their children.

• The most popular is: Don't talk to strangers.

Out of all the population of the United States (about 250

million people), a possible 66 million people are personally acquainted with perhaps an equal number (also 66 million) of other people.

This means that the other 118 million people must be officially classified as Total Strangers.

This is a threatening thought to an adult, and mystifying to a child. He wonders what such an awesomely large segment of the population must *do* with itself in order to keep itself occupied. He knows strangers spend a lot of time wandering the streets, ringing doorbells and asking to read people's gas meters when there aren't any grown-ups home. (They have resolutely tiny, fishlike faces, so that they will look even more peculiar through the little peephole in your front door.) Total Strangers are of course most notorious for parking outside school playgrounds and luring small children to terrible fates.

The two runner-up-most-popular pieces of advice are:

- Sit up straight in your chair.
- Don't talk with pancakes in your mouth.

These are all very good pieces of advice, given by the Clearinghouse of Parents Who Give Advice. You should always follow them.

However, many creative children are skilled in the art of disregarding parental advice, and doing it in a RECOMBINANT FASHION, with interesting results. If, for example, you A) slouch in a chair *and* B) talk to a stranger, C) *with* your mouth full of pancakes, it is scarcely possible that *any* stranger—even a ne'er-do-well sort of stranger—could sustain interest in you for very long. Your parents probably could not *pay* him to sustain interest in you for long.

AN ANTHOLOGY OF MOST-BELOVED THREATS

Mothers usually like to instill things like "economic realities" in you at an early age. They will say things like "Money doesn't grow on trees, Sunny Jim" (which is, at least, something you've been able to substantiate through personal observation). But other times they will make threats to you which will strike you as baroque, at best: "If we spend any more money on toys for you, Biffy," they will say, "we will all have to go to the Poorhouse."

Has anyone ever actually *seen* "the Poorhouse"? Is there a sort of National Poorhouse in Washington, D.C., that you can see on the grand tour, after you have visited the Jefferson Memorial and the Smithsonian? Or are there Regional Poorhouses? How do you *get* to the Poorhouse, if you don't have any money? Can you meet girls at the Poorhouse?

If they really want to threaten you, your parents will remind you of how cushy modern life is. They will tell you about "olden-day" punishments, where sinners were thrown into dungeons and forced to live for days on bread and water. (And it is true that people chained by the wrists in dungeons were never given macadamia-nut ice cream to eat, but on the other hand, they were never given cooked vegetables or liver or baked ham to eat, either.)

MYSTERIES OF THE BODY

Your mother had to have a very powerful knowledge of human anatomy in order to threaten you into staying on the strait-and-narrow. She probably told you Not to Pick at Scabs, because it would result in a Permanent, Disfiguring Scar on your nose or kneecap. (At eight, however, you took this as a positive inducement to do so.) She probably told you that if you crossed your eyes too often, they would stay that way forever. (However, this never prevented entertainers like Frank Fontaine, Charlie Callas, and Alfred E. Neuman from becoming beloved of all Americans.) And she probably also told you that if you ate too fast and swallowed the seeds or pits of fruit, a tree would grow in your stomach. (This is only known to have happened once. A man named Weems in Sonoma County, California, first noticed small branches growing out of his sinuses after swallowing an avocado pit in 1957. He continued to prune back the growth for several years, but died in 1984 when termites invaded his immune system and ate his lungs.)

MAGNUM-FORCE OBEDIENCE

When all else failed, your mother really hit below the belt and resorted to the Biblical scriptures. Not only does she mention that "cleanliness is next to Godliness"; she will strongly intimate that the Last Supper was meant to be the "First of Many Suppers"—only several of the Apostles became unruly and soiled the guest napkins, and the Almighty said, "Okay, that's it! *You're going to make me have to separate you, aren't you?*"

She alone knows that the great Biblical temptress Salome was actually the patron saint of mothers. When Salome performed her Dance of the Seven Veils for King Herod, and they brought her the head of John the Baptist, as she requested, she said, "How many times have I told you? *Put it on a plate!*"

Mothers have been saying this at lunchtime ever since.

To use an emotionally laden expression, it may even seem from all this that mothers are on a kind of "power trip"—dedicated to controlling your brain at all costs from birth to death—and this is, of course, not true, since mothers are also there to protect you and give you dopey advice (which is better than no advice at all when you're down-for-the-count) in times of emotional need. They tell you "There's other fish in the sea," and "They were never worth it anyway," and words to this effect, whenever someone of the opposite sex has just put your heart in the Osterizer and pressed the "PUREE" button. Best of all (and all Moms do this—the ones who don't get their badges revoked), they tell you, "Someday, kid, you'll be able to laugh about this."

Indeed. They never tell you that the "someday" in question only applies if you plan to come back in a future incarnation as a hyena, or a guest on *Hollywood Squares.*

But it's their *job* to keep this bad stuff from you as long as possible.

BEWARE OF FUNNY DAD

Listen to your Mom—she knew why you needed a sense of humor in life. Above all other things, you needed it for the sobering business of living in the same house with your Dad.

There are no good statistics on how many American households are headed by certified Funny Dads. A Funny Dad is not a harmful person—just an INCORRIGIBLE ONE. A Funny Dad never graduates to being a Public Nuisance, because he is much too satisfied being a private one.

He discovered the transcendent humor in hanging you up by your snowsuit on a coat hook the first time you ever went out to a restaurant. (He came back and *got* you. We're not talking about sadism here. Just Statutory Funniness, which is only a misdemeanor in most states.)

Most Funny Dads enjoyed playing practical jokes on your Mom (since it is an interesting and true fact that no Moms in America before 1965 had any sense of humor).

Like, when she would say, "Why don't you eat your chocolate layer cake?" and he would say, "I'm saving it for Ron." And she would say, "Ron who?" and he would say, "Later-Ron" and fall on the floor in convulsions.

And your Mom would always stand there and say, "Oh, Hal, *grow up*." But the point was that no matter how many times your Dad played this joke, your Mom would always say, "Ron who?" even if she was a Vassar graduate and should have known better.

THE THREE AGES AT WHICH YOU KNOW EVERYTHING

It happens at about the age of twelve: you have completed all the human development you ever plan to do, and you spend a lot of your time becoming extremely exasperated, and waiting for this fact to become evident to the people around you.

Being twelve (and knowing everything) is probably the most difficult because you have to endure a lot of relatives telling you almost twenty-four hours a day that you have become Very, Very Big. They say it with an air of reproach, as if Being Big were something you had done specifically To Them.

"LOOK AT HOW BIG SHE IS," they say to each other. "How did she get to be SO BIG?"

This is clearly a rhetorical question; not one to occupy the lab-hours of pituitary scientists. You could say, for example, "I got to be so big because microscopic glands in my lower medulla instructed calcium molecules to deposit themselves in my bone tissue, thereby enlarging my skeletal frame, as well as my joints and connective tissue."

They would slap you around a great deal for being rude and impertinent.

The troublesome thing about grown-ups in general when you are twelve years of age is that they are all inexplicably and monumentally meatheaded about the most obvious things in life. Of course small children often grow up to be large ones. Of course it's "hot enough for you." Of course "it never rains but it pours." You realize the main function of aging is to grow increasingly obtuse as the years go by, and that at the age of twelve you are as mentally developed as you are ever going to be.

But if you are a very well brought-up child, you keep these sad and sobering facts to yourself.

Just for the record, after you are twelve you forget that you know Everything for a few years, until you turn nineteen, at which point you Really Know Everything. Then you forget it all for about fifty-six years, until you turn seventy-five; at which point everyone *admits* that you "Know Everything," but no one wants to listen anymore. This is what makes life so hard.

TAKING CHARGE OF YOUR LIFE

Most children first learn the art of thumbing their nose at authority in secret—the day they learn to put a penny on the railroad tracks and make Abraham Lincoln's face look like a caterpillar. Which leads to the day they discover they can make George Washington's face look like a mushroom by folding a $1 bill. It is *not* inevitable that this sort of behavior will lead to serious character flaws. Call it, if you will, a rite of passage.

But it is also true that at certain crucial "junctures" in the life cycle, life conspires to make you do things you would *almost cetainly eschew* if you had half a brain. It is important to *always do these things,* no matter how stupid and precipitate and pea-headed they make you feel. When your parents took you to the amusement park, there was always a four-foot wooden bunny that said, YOU MUST BE AS TALL AS I AM TO RIDE THE WHIRLING GUT EXPLORER.

And so you lied and sneaked aboard anyway, and afterwards they had to mop up your lunch from the backs of an entire family of eight and several Chevrolet Caprices in the parking lot. You don't know why you did this.

It was simply something that had to be done.

THE MAIN REASON YOU HAVE PARENTS

You cannot, after all, go completely without your parents, because they endowed you with a unique set of "human values," which they labored for an entire generation to acquire. Okay, maybe when you are twelve they strike you as Totally Stupid and Retarded Values. But each family's set of Stupid, Retarded Values is as unique and special as a set of fingerprints.

One mother may say, "You may go out with a short man, as long as he isn't Protestant." Another mother may say, "You should go out with a Catholic woman but make sure she makes her own *ziti.*" As children, we strive to extricate ourselves from our parents' Stupid Values, only to find ourselves hopelessly programmed later in life. "*I* don't know why florists make me nauseous," we say helplessly to our daughters. "Couldn't you go out with a nice car dealer or something?"

Part of the secret of mental health is to *separate* ourselves from our parents. People who are supposed to separate (parents and children) usually stay hopelessly together, and people who are supposed to stay together (husbands and wives) usually become hopelessly separated. This is because no matter how much you love a man or a woman, they are from a Different Family, raised with a whole different set of Stupid, Retarded Values.

What would America be if not for this richness?

The Brain Event: School Lays Claim to America's Minors

THE first thing you learn as a very young child is that there are *rules* to be followed. If you follow the rules, you will be patted on the head, given good grades, and eyed longingly by The College of Your Choice while still in the first grade. (This is what they tell you, at least—for example, behaving yourself in the lunch line can open undreamed-of doors for you. Your first-grade teacher will try to con you into thinking they have tuna scholarships to Harvard. And I am telling you here that they do not.)

But you learn that there are people out there who *never* succeed by following the normal rules, and this is puzzling indeed. You read of examples like Ted Turner, T. Boone Pickens, Lee Iacocca, and, in particular, Prince; and you think, "Can a man not wear heavy eye makeup *and* be the CEO of a major car manufacturer?" and the imagination starts to run rampant.

But first you have to make it through childhood. Which almost always means you have to be promoted to the second grade.

WHAT YOU GO TO SCHOOL FOR

The main reason they make you go to school, and then, eventually, to a place of employment, is so that you will not harbor the delusion that getting up in the morning is somehow optional. (In point of fact, it is *completely* optional, and has been since the days of the Industrial Revolution. The whole *idea* of an Industrial Revolution was to devise enough labor-saving devices so that no one would ever have to get out of bed. For about twelve years after the world was completely mechanized, several people signed on as *contras* in the Industrial Revolution and never got out of bed at all; and what eventually happened was that they never got any mail, and their cats died; but the world as we know it certainly did not come to an end. In fact, the difference between salaried people and self-employed people is that self-employed people actually have to *decide* to get out of bed, and they do it every single day. They never get any medals for this.)

Almost from the very beginning, there is a great deal of censure and ill will directed at children who habitually "oversleep" and "arrive late for school" in the mornings. It is an unforgettable feeling—that moment of opening the door at 9:06 and seeing twenty-five faces turned toward you in rapt attention, as if you were a web-footed Tyrolean circus midget. And the question is not so much whether this attention was lavished on you a lot in childhood, but whether you *enjoyed* it or not. Only the ones who enjoyed it ever turn up on the cover of *Time*.

SCHOOL GIVES YOU REMINISCENCES TO LAST A LIFETIME

Nostalgia organizes itself into nongeometric patterns and shapes. You tend to mark time in elementary school, but not by learning modules, *per se*. You don't remember the exact day you learned to read the way you remember, say, the exact day Richard Matzenberger threw up in Social Studies class, and the janitor got to come in and throw green stuff on it.

You also remember the day you spelled "lixiviate" (on purpose and correctly) for the first and last time in your life. You would have particularly remembered this milestone if you happened to be a boy, because it would have been so rare. *Girls* get a lot of parental reinforcement when they come home having "spelled well" that day. No one ever tells them that no CEO in the Fortune 500 has "spelled" anything in fifteen years. They have divisions that spell for them. *Boys don't "spell."* But this is not a value judgment.

SCHOOL TEACHES YOU "SOCIAL SKILLS"

Incumbent on every school-age youngster is the avoidance of "cooties" and other low-grade playground infections with maximum maintenance of dignity.

It is a sad fact of youth that six-year-olds are seldom represented by legal counsel and are therefore helpless in the face of such accusations as "Ricky has cooties!" and worse.

Children learn witty ripostes to these charges, such as "Liar, liar, pants on fire!" which are skills to last a lifetime.

Like any other social grouping, a school requires a "class system" or else it would collapse inward upon itself. In most towns, such a system is based on looks, muscular coordination, and sheer seniority of residency.

Being a new kid in any school is only slightly less stressful than being a known leper at a Club Med resort. Everything you suspect about the other kids is in fact true: they have all been close personal friends since the fetal stage, they all have better baseball mitts than you do, and they all, for valid sociobiological reasons, dislike you on sight.

When you go home the first day, your mother will invariably say something to you like "Just be yourself and they'll like you." You know that few sane adults would ever be caught dead "being themselves" (hence the invention of

"Dewar's and Soda" and other popular talismans of adulthood), so you cannot really imagine why this particular advice is being palmed off on you.

If you are a bright child the teacher will usually like you, which means that the other kids will instantly initiate the plotting of your untimely death.

If you are an attractive girl, the boys will all like you but the girls will all instantly initiate the plotting of your untimely death.

There are ways out of these dilemmas.

If you are a girl, it is always a good idea to have a number of attractive older brothers, and hold some inaugural "slumber parties" involving a great deal of screaming and use of hair chemicals.

If you are a boy, it can't hurt to take a lot of steroids.

SCHOOL TEACHES RESPONSIBILITY TO YOUTH

In school, there were always kids you liked well enough, until the day they were appointed Hall Monitors.

For reasons you never understood, adult authority figures had chosen these wet-eared young pups to be the dispensers of vigilante justice.

They showed you in the course of Monday–Friday how absolute power corrupted absolutely.

In fact, it is thought that in some progressive schools, the idea of hall monitors was instituted precisely so that the student body could see the workings of a fascist or totalitarian state close up. A sort of hands-on sociology project. In Soviet Russia, up until the early fifties, "Hall Monitors" were trained to shoot to kill, until students without valid bathroom passes were dying in such record numbers that their parents put a stop to the practice.

SCHOOL TEACHES YOU THAT VALID CIVILIZATIONS EXISTED BEFORE YOU WERE BORN, ALTHOUGH THIS IS A TOUGH ONE TO SWALLOW

The worst thing about school was, they invariably wanted to teach you about the Austro-Hungarian Empire on the first day of softball season.

The worst thing about World History in particular is that somebody was always achieving "hegemony" over somebody else. Nobody knows what the word "hegemony" means, or why any empire in its right mind would want to achieve it, but the Austro-Hungarians seemed very keen to achieve it for decades and decades.

Did people go around actively being Austro-Hungarian and liking it? Did they introduce themselves and say, "Hello, I am Fritzi, and Austro-Hungarian?" Did they automatically have better tunics and pastries than we do?

A lot of resourceful children realize that the things we are forced to learn in World History quite simply never happened at all. They tell us, for example, that World War I began when Archduke Ferdinand was assassinated in the streets of Sarajevo by a Serbian with a revolver. But no one on record has any idea what Archduke Ferdinand was archduke of. And there is no such place as Serbia, and there never has been, or it would be somewhere on a map.

Still, it is an essential stretch of the child's imagination to envision a world where these things might actually have happened.

SCHOOL INTRODUCES CHILDREN TO "ABSTRACT THOUGHT"

One of the most confusing developments in English class occurs in about the tenth grade, when they first introduce you to "literary symbolism." Suddenly the teacher tells you that a lot of what you read in nineteenth-century novels actually stands for *something else entirely that isn't even in the book.* The whale in *Moby-Dick* isn't really "a whale." *Everything* in *The Scarlet Letter* is symbolic—the trees and the fields and Hester Prynne's name spelled backwards ("Ennyrp Retseh"), and so on.

It is troublesome for young girls to read Nathaniel Hawthorne and be told the true meaning of *The Scarlet Letter.* If a woman wears a big red "A" on her chest, it means she is a sinner and an adulteress. If a man wears a big red "A" on his chest, it means he is a second-round draft choice for the Houston Astros.

Suddenly we go around asking questions like "Is all of life symbolic? Does 'foreshadowing' really mean something? Should I worry, the next time I have to fly, if there is a guy with a black hood and a scythe standing at the departure lounge at O'Hare?"

Higher mathematics is another discipline that teaches abstract throught. Every useful thing you learn in math you learn by the fourth grade, which gives you plenty of time to forget it in the years to come. And then, in about the eighth grade, many students learn that there is more to math than just Numbers. There are Odd and Even Numbers; Negative Numbers; Logarithmic Functions; there are even Real and *Imaginary* Numbers. There are Binary Number Systems where things tend to add up to apocalyptic totals like 1001010010111100010 and worse. (Is this useful for adult life? Will the IRS accept it if you figure out your taxable income in imaginary numbers?)

It is, unfortunately, the nature of "abstract thought" that it is not up to you to discover the virtue or value of learning it. It is too abstract for this.

THE BOTTOM LINE ABOUT SCHOOL

Since you will have spent *a full one-sixth* of your life (the shining, most precious, most ephemeral, most irreplaceable years) in school, then you may as well have gotten yourself what is known as "Decent Grades," because God knows "grades" are fraught with a lot more symbolism than just a letter on a page.

Don't kid yourself here.

Savants argue that there is such a thing as a LIFETIME GRADE-POINT: A lifelong aura that hangs over all humans and is as unmistakable as strong perfume. (In fact, a guy in a bar only asks you "What's your sign?" because he doesn't *have* to ask "What's your grade-point?" There are "A+" fingernails and "B−" fingernails. There are "A−" throaty laughs and "B+" throaty laughs. There are solid-"C" dates, who everyone says have "a nice personality," but everyone permanently loses their phone numbers. The worst thing to be is a "D," because it usually means you aspired to being an "F"—a sort of cross between John Hinckley and Joan Collins—but you've never pulled it off.)

No one disputes that Diane Sawyer is an "A" and Phyllis George is a "B." No one disputes that the entire Osmond family is a "C+," whether they own most of Utah or not.

Adolescence: Or, "Who Are You and What Are You Doing in My Skin?"

EVERY girl has asked herself and her friends the question "What if I am getting dressed for gym and there is a fire drill and I am in my underpants?" Most normally developed twelve-year-old girls would choose to stay inside and die in the flames rather than run out of the school in their underpants in front of the principal and the boys' shop class.

And most of the boys in the boys' shop class would choose to stay inside and die in the flames if the girls' gym class would promise just once to run outside the school dressed in their underpants.

This is a sign of normal human development.

It is terribly difficult being at what everyone calls "a difficult age."

There is, for example, the ever-present threat of "Sudden Adolescent Growth Spurts"—ugly and unique afflictions that can make us as much as *a foot taller* during adolescence than we will be as adults.

At an early age your mother probably sat you down and told you it wasn't external fripperies that counted in a person, or chiseled features, or cheekbones like Nefertiti's, but rather something called "inner beauty." (And you thought, "Either Mom is a liar, or someone is paying Estée Lauder $16 million a year for nothing." And in fact, both these things are true. Such is the exquisite duality of life.)

THE DAWN OF TRUE AGONY

At the age of fifteen, most adolescents are biologically capable of luring mates, becoming fecund, and repopulating the globe many, many times over. Clearly, this is a major planning and zoning error on the part of the Almighty, and He saw it coming and realized He'd have to keep the various sexes locked in their bathrooms long enough to forestall a disaster.

And so He invented Serious Acne.

Serious Acne means that God is borrowing your face for a while and using it for various seismic studies of the sebaceous glands. If a fifteen-year-old's face were blown up to the size of South America, his pores would and could erupt energetically enough to bury Lima and many parts of western Venezuela.

It only *seems* like each individual case of acne lasts for ninety-three thousand years and requires enough Benzoyl Peroxide to fill the Grand Canyon, and that your nose and forehead alone excrete enough oil to be considered voting members of OPEC.

No one case of acne lasts forever. (Okay, one of them once did, but the odds are in your favor that no one with zits will be likely to have to collect Social Security.)

A lot of teenagers take to the beach, figuring that the sun will camouflage God's grossest handiwork. But of course, the sun is something you really can't win with these days. It's true that if you stay out of it entirely, you look like you died two weeks ago and no one attractive will ever want to marry you. But if you go out in it too much, all the magazines tell you you will reach the age of twenty-five looking like Miss Lillian Carter, or the Chief Monk in *Lost Horizon.* In other words, *if you are not George Hamilton, do not try this at home.*

At least boys and men have the option of growing beards, sideburns, mustaches, and eyebrows to cover a host of skin ailments, but facial hair has a serious disadvantage. For every year that a beard remains on your face, *your actual chin will recede a full inch*; and if you shave off a beard you've had more than five years, your own family will not recognize you and will run screaming from the room.

THE NEXT CRISIS

Usually, as a teenager, you have a grace period (about two weeks) between the time you stop worrying about your skin and the time you start worrying about being blimpo. (Or sometimes it's fatness first, then skin. No one wins this one. No one ever has.)

Study after study shows that in modern, mechanized America, 75 percent of the population is seriously overweight, and in earlier civilizations, there had simply been no precedent for this statistic. It is known that in past civilizations, 56 percent of the populations worked as serfs and slaves and were regularly and strenuously flogged, which was considered to be an AEROBIC ACTIVITY, and none of these people ever had to cut out starches or invest in an Exercycle.

It is as a child and adolescent that you first become fascinated by Miracle Weight Loss Diets that you see pictured on the back of women's magazines. Here are human beings the size of tour buses or commercial zeppelins, and in the "after" pictures, they look like Don Knotts. They took a MIRACLE PILL. (In the less-expensive popular magazines, the "before" and "after" pictures are not always quite so dramatic. But without exception, the people in the "after" pictures have greatly improved *hairstyles*.)

THE CURSE OF FREEDOM

Everywhere you look in adolescence, there are unquestionably Restraints in life. Your parents, for example, have probably invested in "orthodontia," a sort of police-state-of-the-mouth, where your front teeth are made an offer they can't refuse by a megastructure of wires and hooks and metal.

This is why LEARNING TO DRIVE ANY AMERICAN OR FOREIGN-MADE AUTOMOBILE represents the ultimate freedom, and the chance to get "over the wall."

Even though driving is the most important activity Americans can ever learn, *all driving instructors look like loan enforcers for the mob.* And yet, how can we ever remunerate our driving instructors enough for the selfless service they perform for all living beings?

It is the job of the driving instructor to explain that the concept of "limited-access highways" was invented to keep you personally off the road.

"Use your mirrors. I do not see you using your mirrors," the instructor says, using the mirror to adjust his hairpiece.

Always kiss the hem of your driving instructor's garment. You will make the valuable "points" that you can always use when you pass on to the Great Beyond or other, comparable situations.

OTHER MOMENTS OF TRUTH

It is generally accepted that adolescence is the time a person wrestles to pull something called a "personality" out of the screeching mass of sameness that surrounds him. We read in the various popular magazines that it is advisable for "young adults" to have a "personal style," and we are constantly nagged by the fear that we haven't got one.

Personal style seems to involve things like piercing one ear, and wearing berets (a dead giveaway), and calling our parents "Chuck and Debra" (regardless of what their names may actually be). We know that our clothing should be "making a statement," but we fear that it is only "posing a query"—and not a very direct one, at that.

But there is an even more pressing task in late adolescence: we need to decide "what we want to be when we grow up." We need to do this primarily because *anything* is better than *not* deciding what we want to be, which is known in many circles as "graduate school."

In Europe this process is more scientific. If you fail your *baccalaureate* at age fifteen, they say, "Okay, Sven, we guess you are going to be a stevedore."

No one in Europe bombs on their College Boards and gets to hitchhike to Idaho to get their heads on straight.

But seriously—what is the age when your destiny reveals itself to you? When G. Gordon Liddy was a child, for example, he roasted a rat and ate it. This told his parents immediately that someday he would break into Democratic National Committee headquarters, or else become *sous-chef* at a Roy Rogers restaurant.

Most of us do not see the future with nearly this kind of clarity. So rather than sit around guessing, they (whoever "they" are) invented the Scholastic Aptitude Test. It is not known why everyone dreads SATs as teenagers but then, years later, seems to enjoy playing the game of Trivial Pursuit as adults, even though Trivial Pursuit is an SAT test in disguise—except that nobody ever sends your Trivial Pursuit scores to five Major Ivy League Universities.

The Bad Stuff

A Short History of Intergalactic Bad Luck

SOMETIMES it helps to realize that you are not the only human being on the third planet from the sun, whizzing through space at the rate of 98,860 feet per second with no braking capacity, and no Power of Appeal when the world is Not Your Oyster or any other high-priced shellfish on any particular morning.

Early man did not catch on to this truth.

The first man to view a solar eclipse thought that the sun was going away permanently because it was in a snit about something he (man) had done. *Sure,* the sun, which is a cosmic entity 864,424 miles in diameter, is going to sit up there in the sky and say, "Okay, I am *annoyed* because some pin-sized life form three planets to the left of here disemboweled a *goat* wrong. . . . I am going to take a hike because a couple of Mayans down in proto-Mexico didn't build a couple *pyramids* high enough. I've got nothing *better* to do. . . ."

It is a good exercise in cosmic humility to watch a solar eclipse if you can—remembering that every fifth-grade teacher since the Stone Age has recommended that you *only do this with a bag over your head.* This is sure to impress your neighbors, although it won't quite answer your near-term questions about existence.

THE UNIVERSE DEFIES NEW JERSEY WOMAN— NO END IN SIGHT!

The universe has let us down so often, it's no wonder we rarely believe its idle, piddling promises anymore.

A lot of people had been keeping themselves alive with vitamin supplements for the last seventy-six years, waiting for the next occurrence of Halley's Comet. And then when it finally occurred, you couldn't even see it with the naked eye unless you woke up at five o'clock in the morning; and a lot of people kicked up a general nuisance about this and demanded refunds.

Even black holes are not living up to the impressive ink they were getting ten or twelve years ago. Certainly when they were first theorized about, in the late sixties, they scared and impressed a number of us; here was a sort of inverted NON-THING that behaved like a kind of giant Electrolux in space, and could scarf down Pluto for breakfast, and spit out the moons of Saturn as if they were cherry pits, and ALL OF EARTH would have been history before you could say "Peloponnesian Wars 431–404 B.C."

But then the entire "Black Hole Experience" was cheapened when a lot of eighth-graders tried to use them as the reason for the disappearance of their homework assignments. (A lot of people have in fact tragically vanished into black holes; TV's original "Partridge Family" disappeared into one in 1973.)

THE EARTH AND US; PERSONAL FRIENDSHIP OR TWISTED VENDETTA?

Every time a major disaster hits some part of the world we live in, we are understandably relieved to hear that it only affected 1 million people in a trailer park in Bangladesh, and that no one from the Tri-County or Metropolitan Area was involved.

Most of the bad things that happen in America seem to do so independently of waterspouts or rocks or long-term meteorology; but this, of course, cannot be the case for all eternity. We are living in a comfortable little bookshelf in the wall unit of geologic time. We never think that the entire North American continent is a series of *tectonic plates* that can come apart at the edges without so much as a howdy-do. (Yes, the popular MOUNT ST. HELENS did kill about sixty-three people in 1980, but they were non–lava-resistant; so we cannot, as we so often do, *blame the volcano.*)

Aside from not building microsurgery clinics on top of the San Andreas Fault, we tend to say Ho-ho-ho to the thought of TOTAL GEOLOGIC DEVASTATION. When someone like producer IRWIN ALLEN makes a movie about it, we say, "Ho-ho-ho, that *alarmist auteur* Irwin Allen!" The citizens of greater Pompeii went around saying Ho-ho-ho, up until the moment they were eating airborne cinders the size of Volkswagens for breakfast.

No, nothing *major* has happened in geologic time for about nine million years or so, so ladies and gentlemen, WE ARE DUE FOR A BIGGIE.

The atmospheric "ozone" problem is but a mere one. Our earth is heating up like gangbusters; our icecaps are fizzing like Alka-Seltzer. The damage has been done. In the years 1956–1962, so many Americans used aerosol products that the ozone layer was depleted beyond hope, and only a thin, saving wisp of the stuff is left to protect humanity.

- On June 9, 1956, so many women in Twinsburg, Ohio, sprayed their hair on their way to a bingo match that the sea level will rise 3 feet by 1989, and drown Belgium.
- So many women have used Butter-Flavored Pam in their cooking that by the early twenty-first century, the Bay of Biscay will have enveloped all the low-lying "prime tourist destinations" of the Balearic Islands.
- So much Right Guard aerosol was sold in one week in Augusta, Georgia, that in 2009, Lake Superior will evaporate.

It is perhaps the Japanese who have posed the most provocative question of all: with the world ecosystem in the wacky state it's in, what is to prevent the dinosaurs from deciding that the experience of being "extinct" was *unfulfilling*? In several futurist Japanese films, the dinosaurs have come back, to great acclaim, and knocked down tiny scale models of the city of Tokyo—but the producers realized too late that three thousand tiny servings of shrimp tempura would not sustain them, so they sadly let them become extinct again by the end of the movie.

Slam-Dancing with Destiny

YOU probably know a bit about the mathematics of bad luck, whichever end of the scale you fall on. It's absolutely true, for instance, that all bad things come in multiples of three.

If you've had a particularly bad week, and you've had two major disasters (or five, or eight), you may as well make yourself a cup of coffee and wait in your living room for the next one. In fact, if the next disaster doesn't hit you pretty quickly, you should take matters into your own hands and immediately set fire to your rug or house. Why wait around to see what Fate has in store for you? It's like ordering the house dressing at a cheap restaurant.

A lot of people save time and energy by visualizing all the things that could go wrong in their lives and worrying about them long in advance. The post office says "Mail early," doesn't it?

It pays to WORRY EARLY.

- If you are a student, you *know* who is going to get called on to stand up and recite "The Wreck of the Hesperus" aloud when you were up all the night before reading Archie & Veronica comics.
- If you have children, you *know* that if one of your children gets bitten by a dog and you take her to the doctor's, there is a 45-percent probability that your remaining two children will set fire to their hands with a cigarette lighter while waiting in the car.
- If the news says, EXPLODING MOVING VAN PLUNGES OFF EMBANKMENT ON THE OHIO TURNPIKE, you know it will be the one Mayflower truck in America with all *your* earthly possessions inside.

THE WAGES OF MISFORTUNE

Unfortunately, you cannot get paid to have bad luck—as you could in the 1950s, when *Queen for a Day* was on TV. It went off the air, owing to a streak of . . . well, bad luck. But creative Americans have long recognized the intrinsic Entertainment Value of bad luck.

This is why we like to celebrate a highly unusual holiday on the first of April, known as "April Fools' Day"—a day of very much mirth and jocularity, where one highly humorous person calls up a close friend on the phone and says, *"Guess what! Your dog has died."* Then the friend becomes extremely sad about this and begins to cry, and then the "jokester" waits a minute and says, "Guess what! *Your dog did not really die.*"

It is, of course, not immediately evident why many Americans roll with laughter in the retelling of such pranks. ("*I wish I had seen your face.* Especially when I described how Sparky looked under the wheels of that *86-ton semi*!")

In grappling with fate, it may help to know that there are only two major types of disasters you will ever encounter: AN ACT OF GOD (as in fire, flood, pestilence, and so on) and AN ACT OF "JERKS" (as in "people who were put on this Earth specifically to torment you personally, and seem to serve no other useful function whatsoever").

JERKS AND YOU

In the beginning, God created the heaven and the earth, and on the seventh day everyone knows He rested, but on the eighth day, for reasons known to Him alone, God created "jerks."

No one really knows why the Almighty felt the need to do this thing. It was, no doubt, during the time when the earth was without form, and void, and the Almighty was getting a little slaphappy, and so he invented "jerks" to entertain

Him. The theory probably was the Almighty could just sort of walk away from the "jerks" when they ceased to amuse Him. But He had some kind of change of heart about man, and He suddenly blurted out, "Listen, how would you like to work in an office with these 'jerks' I've created?" and man said, "Why, Lord?" and the Lord said, "Builds character."

And so the five-day work week was invented (with the "jerks" getting to take more sick days).

Something went wrong, though, when the "jerks" began to appear in all walks of life. And indeed, today they are with us everywhere.

Now is the time to take a little guided tour of the "World of Jerks," just to see what makes them tick, and where we can best expect them to turn up.

People Who Work in Supermarkets

No one in America should ever attempt to grocery-shop without a degree in marketing, nutrition, and martial arts.

In France they are monstrously casual about things like shopping. They carry around tiny bags made of string and say things like "Oh, Jean-Pierre, look at that little rabbit in the window. *Let's take it home and poach it,*" and then they go to the *cinéma* and watch a Jerry Lewis movie.

The best way to drive around a modern American supermarket parking lot is with a military-surplus armored personnel carrier, several rounds of ammo, and three or four Dobermans *trained to maim.* And still, you haven't even made it inside the store yet.

The famous inventor who invented the shopping cart died recently, so probably no one will ever know how to remove one shopping cart from a long line of shopping carts. But provided you do make it inside the supermarket with your cart, and have made it alive past the "KISS THE BUTCHER" sign and the volunteer ladies trying to get you to buy Spam *au gratin* canapés, you have plenty of time to stop and contemplate the eternal question WHERE DO THEY FIND THE PEOPLE WHO WORK IN SUPERMARKET CHECK-OUT LINES?

One theory is that they are members of a LOST CIVILI-

ZATION WHERE NORMAL HAND–EYE COORDINATION IS UNKNOWN. They ask questions like "Hey, LaWanda—is 'Love My Carpet' a meat item or a vegetable?"

You always seem to have staggered into their line with the *one item* that is so strange and fantastical, they have *never seen it before* in their all-too-abbreviated lives and they turn it over and over with their manicured little hands, in the vast wonderment of their discovery. When you grasp them by the uniform and yell, "It's called *canned corn,* bird-brain!" their eyes focus on you ever-so-gradually, and they say, "You gotta get that check approved at the manager's."

Many of them are not content to stay put working at checkout lines and have secret dreams of becoming toll-booth attendants.

Unhappily for us, many of their dreams come true.

The U.S. Postal Service

We tend to denigrate the employees of the U.S. Postal Service as being stupid or backward people. In fact, many of these people are struggling along on Guggenheim fellowships, and are grappling with loftier concerns than whether your mail reaches you when you would like it to. Many of them are free-lance "philosophy technicians," who have proved, again and again, that "truth is stranger than fiction."

Do you ever wonder what happens to a letter that you have just put in the mailbox? First of all, the letters are "collected" at "regular intervals."

Then comes the important part. All the letters (or "mail," as they are called) are sent to a large room to be sorted. Sorting is an important part of mail delivery. The mail is separated into piles. All the letters with typewritten addresses go into one pile. There is a pile for all the letters to ZIP Code 10570. There is a pile for 44139. Then there is a pile for all the other ZIP Codes in the world. There is a pile for all mail labeled "NO POSTAGE NECESSARY IF MAILED IN THE UNITED STATES." These letters are shredded, since they bear no postage.

There is a pile for all mail that needs to be "forwarded to

a new address." What this means is that all the mail handlers get together and discuss whether they *want* to deliver this mail to the address in question. Then all the letters that the Post Office cannot condone are shredded in the shredder.

Then a large electric fan is brought into the room and all the letters are blown against the wall at an extremely high velocity.

You may be shocked to read a lot of these things, but studies have shown that if the majority of our postal workers did not have these strange activities to entertain them, they could become bored, indifferent, inefficient, and worse.

Exterminators

People who choose to become professional exterminators were invariably called "Lumpy" in junior high school.

They have lungs of staggering capability. They are able to inhale gases that would kill a herd of airborne rhinos, and live. In fact, if an exterminator inhales anything that has more than 50 percent of normal oxygen, he becomes extremely light-headed and has to lie down for a few hours.

When you get exterminators on the phone, and tell them you have bugs, the first thing they usually do is laugh. They can afford to do this because they, along with morticians, will always be in a seller's market, and they know it and you know it and laughing at you on the phone is a way of keeping you in on this news.

Then you make the mistake of asking how much they charge for "a visit." This really makes them laugh a lot. No exterminator, like no postman, ever rings less than twice. He will tell you more than you ever want to know about insect courtship and reproduction cycles, the upshot being that one visit is sure to take care of the bugs, and another visit will take care of the bug offspring. (By the third visit, since they have already killed off the cats and dogs that brought the insects into the house in the first place, you have a reasonably good chance of never seeing the bugs again.)

Most exterminators advertise that they come in "unmarked vans." This is because an exterminator was once sued for painting on the side of his truck, *"ON MY WAY TO REMOVE DISGUSTING VERMIN FROM THE HOME OF MRS. BETTEJANE MCNAMARA, 35 WINDWHISTLE DRIVE, HIGHLAND PARK, MICHIGAN. 313-555-2705."*

Hotel Employees

Hotel employees do not, as a rule, wear badges identifying them as "jerks." Their badges almost always identify them as *"KIRK BRADY. HOW MAY I ASSIST YOU?"*

When you meet a hotel receptionist for the first time, he always lets you know, via an incredibly subtle display of facial English, that his hotel is temporarily lowering its long tradition of impeccable standards by allowing someone of your ilk to occupy one of its beds even for a fleeting period. You can never prove in a court of law that hotel employees are being unkind to you. At the very best, State's Attorneys have only been able to get convictions along the lines of "premediated superciliousness" and "condescension in the third degree."

The minute the hotel porter has rounded the corner with your baggage (which by International Hotel Law may *only* make its way to your room by way of the 19th floor, the 20th floor, and 21st floor, and the Catering Department), the entire staff begins to recognize and act on its Unique Responsibility: the important business of informing all friends and relatives who call you with urgent, life-threatening messages, that:

A) no one with your name has checked in yet, or

B) someone with your name checked out yesterday morning, or

C) the hotel is not allowed by law to have any record of what room you might presently be occupying.

Hotel receptionists are required to at least approximate a mien of human kindness unless for some reason you approach them with the information that you would like to be "moved." ("Hi, the wall is missing from my room" is not an acceptable reason for wanting to move.) The hotel receptionist (the identical twin sister of yesterday's "KIRK BRADY") will politely tell you that the hotel is "fully booked" this evening. Even though you have seen with your own eyes that every room on the fifth floor is presently occupied by members of the female janitorial staff watching *Search for Tomorrow.*

Maybe you have seen the television show about the staff of a hotel (known as *Hotel*). There is a blond actress named Heidi on the show who plays a hotel receptionist who is a genuinely kind human being.

She is the greatest actress on earth.

Institutions of Lending

Maybe you have gotten one of those rose-scented love letters from *your* bank lately.

"Dear PREFERRED CUSTOMER," they say.

"We are sending you this letter because you are one of our best, most reliable depositors—and also because we like you personally, for who you really and truly are, and as a genuine, feeling human being. We sometimes cannot stop thinking about you in the middle of the night; the thought of your money down in our vaults makes us feel warm and happy inside.

"We would like you to visit us more often, and bring many more large sacks of your money, so that we can become truly close—perhaps closer than any human being and Financial Institution have ever been before. Don't let us down. Our doors will be open to you from 9 A.M. until exactly 3 P.M., after which our security guards will draw their weapons; but you know you have our eternal love, respect, accrued interest, and devotion. . . ."

Missives like these, of course, send us flocking down to the First National at the first available opportunity. But of course, *most* of the transactions we perform at the bank are simple day-to-day "cash-window functions," and you may have noticed something somewhat disillusioning.

It is a rule in life that most professional people like you do their banking on their lunch hours—*and most professional bank tellers do their lunching on their bank hours.*

This is why there is usually one bank teller per eighty-five customers in any bank between the hours of 12 and 1—and he is usually on the phone to Maintenance, trying to get his cash drawer unstuck. Whenever you finally do reach the front of the bank line, all the tellers immediately decide to make long-distance phone calls, and they will not make eye contact with you, even if you jump up and down and frantically wave your arms. (Which will also cause the security guard to draw his gun and escort you out. Even as he escorts you out, none of the tellers will look at you. Bank tellers are trained at the same School of Avoiding Eye Contact as are professional waiters and waitresses.)

Yes, it can be disillusioning to become "involved" with YOUR BANK. To realize that you were lured down to your local branch with blandishments and idle flattery and fervent promises. You feel used. Exploited. Cheapened.

You're wrong here, of course. If you really came as cheap as all that, how many banks would bother with you?

The Department of Motor Vehicles

Of course, if you listened to the voice of reason, you would never get behind the wheel of an automobile for any purpose. (Unless you are someone like Jackie Stewart, who has managed to stay out of fiery collisions long enough to do TV endorsements for paste wax, although all those years of pent-up high-speed stress have made his speaking voice extremely squeaky. If you had any brains at all, this would be a warning to you to obey speed limits.)

Driving is dangerous, hazardous, perilous, and dangerous. In fact, if no one ever drove, *most American transportation deaths would occur in plane crashes, where they belong.*

But ironically, even though most American marriages are even greater disasters than most American car crashes, it is still much easier to get a marriage license than a driver's license.

If you call the Department of Motor Vehicles in your state to ask them how to go about applying for a license, THERE IS NO POSSIBLE WAY THAT THE CORRECT INFORMATION WILL BE DIVULGED TO YOU.

Most State Departments of Motor Vehicles employ PROFESSIONAL HUMORISTS to man their offices and answer their telephones for them. They will tell you that you need two pieces of I.D., but they will not mention that their offices will be closed between 10 A.M. and 4 P.M., and that you need valid proof of birth. (Many criminals who have never been born have tried to apply for driver's licenses, causing untold clerical damage, as well as serious loss to life and limb.)

It is almost never possible to handle any important DMV business over the telephone. The DMV likes to see you on the premises, in the flesh, because, much like your Personal Banker, the DMV wants you to prove you really care about It.

The DMV offers you a series of "lines" to stand in upon your arrival, which are often color-coded, and labeled with such legends as "RENEWAL," "NON-RENEWAL," "EYE TEST," "FIRST OFFENDERS," "WRITTEN TEST," "ROAD TEST APPOINTMENTS," "PREFERRED DRIVERS," "OUT-OF-STATE," "ILLEGAL ALIENS," and others. It will also notify you which pertinent documents you will need to stand in which line, *leaving out one crucial document,* so that you will have to either A) go home, or B) stand in another line until the DMV closes for the day.

If you arrive at the head of the line with all the pertinent documents, the person behind the counter will become very much upset because you are not playing according to the rules. He will then request that you have one or all of the following:

- Social Security card or military I.D.
- Department-store charge card
- Birth certificate or passport
- Previously issued operator's license
- Official team photo of the 1965 Boston Celtics, including Bob Cousy
- Perfect attendance record from eighth or ninth grade

All of this is handled with perfect taste, discretion, and patience by the DMV personnel, but there are always incidents of individuals screaming and setting fire to themselves on DMV premises, and this of course ruins things for all the rest of us.

IS THERE HOPE FOR THE JERKS OF SOCIETY?

Many people know they will never truly be successful in life, primarily *because* they are jerks. There are *options* for these people. The FBI has even instituted a "Jerk Re-Location Program," whereby known offenders are sent to new towns, given a fresh start, and assigned a "new identity." (Applicants look through a catalogue and say, "I would like to be a chiropractor," "I would like to be makeup artist," or "I would like to be 'Mr. T.' ") Many jerks become extremely religious and choose to be "born again," although it was clearly a very bad idea in the first place.

Many of them become Country & Western singers.

However, none of them, at a cellular level, can ever really change.

A FINAL WORD OF WARNING

There are many people among us who are not quite spectacularly harmful, but are skilled in the art of minor annoyance and low-grade aggravation.

They are known to us variously as the "Rude," the "Loud," the "Tactless," the "Morning Deejays," and the "Simply Congenitally Irritating."

Rudeness, in particular, has received mixed reviews in recent society. We do not seem to be able to deal with it in a consistent, levelheaded, and universally agreed-on fashion. Why, for example, are there separate sections in restaurants for people who smoke cigarettes, but no special sections for people who talk with food on their faces? (Many Washington legislators have been recorded talking with mayonnaise on their faces, which is why it is so difficult to get a federal ruling on this issue.)

Why are there no special sections on buses and in doctors' waiting rooms for people who snap their chewing gum? Why are there no special "Talking in an Obnoxious Voice About the Stock Market" cars on the Metro-North New Haven Line?

One way of picking out "Simply Irritating People" in a crowd is that they have certain trademark ways of beginning sentences. For example, they very often say, "If you want to know *my* opinion . . ." (People who begin sentences with "If you want to know *my* opinion" never wait for an informal ballot, or for a show of hands, before proceeding.)

Many Irritating People begin sentences with *"I mean this sincerely,"* or *"Can I give you a piece of advice?"* or *"I really can't believe I'm telling you this."* (In nine out of ten cases, unfortunately, neither can you.)

A corollary to this is the practice of wrapping up an argument or particularly annoying tirade with the phrase "Yeah, well, at least I'm being *honest* about this." There is something about uttering these words (however accurate they may be) which makes people's voices shoot up about five octaves, and their breathing become shallow and irregular. And the point is that there is no record anywhere that being furnished with "honest" but horrible information has ever done anyone any good.

There is a little bony cabinet in your brain where you carry around all the information known as "the truth," and you spend your whole life trying to keep that information contained, so that it won't poison everything else you've got going on.

How can you avoid Congenitally Irritating People as much as possible and lead a full, rich, productive life?

Well, believing that you can succeed in avoiding these people makes about as much sense as believing that all Professional Real Estate Agents are telling you the truth; and that they would all like to be your personal friend and drive you around in their cars for the rest of their lives.

Arranging never to leave your home is only an intermittently successful strategy. Jerks have your phone number and they will not hesitate to use it.

But screaming very occasionally into the telephone mouthpiece is probably good for your endocrine system.

Money, Work, and You: Pretty Much in That Order

A man stood on a Philadelphia street corner in 1969 and said the words "I hardly ever think about money." There were a great many people present, including sound technicians, video crews, and newspaper reporters, because THIS WAS THE LAST TIME IN AMERICAN HISTORY THAT ANYONE EVER SAID THESE WORDS.

There are some who believe that a mysterious "hand of mischief" came along and wiped "greed" off the list of "Seven Deadly Sins"—and replaced it with "taking full vacation time."

The basis of the American economy seems to be YOU MUST WORK VERY HARD, and you will either A) have very much money to show for it, or B) at least have the pleasure of "having worked very hard" for nothing, which is more than most "Eastern Bloc bureaucrats" can say. (They also have nothing, but are denied the pleasure of having worked very hard for it.)

Lately, however, there have been rumblings and statistics that have us all more than a little worried.

AMERICA "IN THE RED"

Every year, the so-called "National Debt" mounts further up into the trillions of dollars—more money than most of us will ever see in our lives. And the issue of "Who" we even owe all this money to is shaky, at best. How did we let it get away from us in the first place? Did we *think* before we spent all this money? Did we spend it on *shoes* and *fast living*? Do we really owe the Kingdom of Norway 194,000 kroner's worth of back kippers, and did we expect them not to *notice* that all this piscine currency is missing?

The thought of all this "National Debt" is frightening because we were brought up to believe that the United States has more money than God. As a nation, we have collectively earned enough money to buy a 340,000-foot Geoffrey Beene ranch mink evening stole for the Statue of Liberty to wear on dates, but we *still don't seem to know where all this money is.*

The idea of "credit" has made "real money" such an abstraction that you have to be a licensed metaphysicist even to discuss it in public. And this kind of cavalier attitude is "trickling down" to the average citizen in disturbing ways.

There is a bizarre new money disorder making the rounds which clinicians are at a loss to explain in the medical and financial journals.

Many women fall prey each year to this disorder, similar to "Somnambulism," or "Sleepwalking," and known as "Sleep *Shopping*"—wherein they rise from their beds, remove their credit cards from their purses, go on three- and four-hour shopping binges, and afterwards have *no recollection of what they have done*; and yet the record of their crimes shows up on their monthly statement. "I have not been to a store in *months*," they say in horror, "and yet my Bloomingdale's statement says *ninety-nine thousand dollars.* Did *I* buy that cabin cruiser? Did I buy sixty-three Christian Dior brassieres on sale? Did I buy that tube of Italian moisturizer that cost $690.38?"

A COURSE IN ECONOMICS THAT OUGHT TO EXPLAIN THE WHOLE THING PRETTY NEATLY

Trying to understand Advanced Economics is not a very good idea for amateurs. What we on earth seem to "do" better than anyone else in the galaxy is Traffic in Commodities. There are "commodities" out there *everywhere* serving as the building blocks of commerce and civilization: Aluminum and *M*agnesium and *E*lectrical parts and *R*utabagas and *I*ce cubes and *C*orn cribs and *A*irplane parts . . . put them all together and they would make a very big mess all over the floor of the Chicago Mercantile Exchange, but they would also somehow spell out "America." *(Try* it—put those letters together and *do it.)*

Nowadays, the list of things that could legitimately be labeled "commodities" has become vast and wondrous to behold. Presently, we can legally buy and sell "bright ideas," "American know-how," kisses, "options," and third basemen; "half-baked ideas" and (this may be redundant) "film treatments"; "gift certificates" and "T-bills"; "Pasts" *(My Father, Frank Sinatra)* and "Futures" ("My One True Love: Prudential-Bache"). We can buy and sell TIME ITSELF (since time is "money," less time is more money; "quality" "parenting" time is worth more than "parents-who-are-still-married-to-each-other" time). Not least of all is time *sharing* —the successful grafting of "time itself" (almost always invisible) onto "real estate" (usually equally invisible) to create a product which has left a great many people happy and fulfilled, although nobody really knows why, and nobody dares to ask.

Take an aspirin immediately. This is going to get worse before we get to the happy part again. *Get rid of that Tylenol! Do you still have that stuff in the house?*

Nowadays, there are "inequities" in the "flow structure" of the American economic system that many of us are all-too-painfully aware of:

We of some affluence know—or can imagine—the feeling of being approached from behind on a dark spring evening and asked to Surrender All Our Money. No explanations, no chance to cry out or summon aid, no sense of human dignity; just "Give it up, *now*." It is indeed a unique feeling of senselessness and waste and rage. . . .

And yet this, in a nutshell, is what The Annual Income Tax Experience is all about.

A lot of people have complained about being in the "effective-50-percent" or "75-percent" tax bracket, but some of us have made THE QUANTUM LEAP INTO THE 200-PERCENT TAX BRACKET. Each year, we owe the government more money than we will ever make in our whole lives.

We will never know what we did to deserve this.

Perhaps if you have ever witnessed TV's lovely VANNA WHITE, spinning TV's famous WHEEL OF FORTUNE, sending thousands of prizes, cash, and free gifts into the laps of lucky, RANDOMLY CHOSEN contestants, you have some idea of how the Internal Revenue Service operates.

Only in reverse.

This is one of the many reasons for the inventions of "Over-the-Counter Sleep Aids," and other products of their ilk.

A MAJOR PITFALL

The world is divided up into two kinds of people: those who pay their bills, taxes, and library fines on time, and those who say, "Try and find me, *Federales Pig-Dogs*!"

For some reason, those who never pay their bills rarely get caught. They usually manage to strike crude oil while laying a new garage foundation and go to live in Brazil and build condos for war criminals, and live happily ever after.

This is why the government and other creditors feel the need to lean on you personally, since you are all too easy to cheaply locate.

The more you conscientiously pay your bills, the more "they" will track you down and tell you you never paid your bills at all, and that you have got to be kidding when you say you paid your bills, when the records show you never did anything of the sort.

Then you send them a XEROX of the check you sent them, and they say, "Forget it. This is your FINAL NOTICE, hotdog."

So you send them your fingerprints, a COLOR XEROX of the check stub, a small bribe, and a Christmas card.

And they say, "Very good move, Jack. This is *America.* People like you are making this system *stink.*"

You send them a Polaroid of your kids and a Promissory Note, and they say, "We're coming for your car. We're coming for your *family.* We're coming for your *pets.*"

PERSONAL FINANCE: ONE PRACTICAL APPROACH

PROCRASTINATION is a fairly useful invention, probably devised by the Stygians in the fifteenth century. Procrastination, simplified, is a way of putting a glove on the fickle finger of fate. Or actually, a large fur mitten. There isn't anyone in the world who doesn't procrastinate, although lots of books have been written to try to get you to stop. No one knows why anyone writes, or finishes, these books.

And one thing is true: the longer you put something off, the more odious and hateful it turns out to be. All you have to do is sit down and take a brave little stab at balancing your checkbook to realize you had a very good reason for putting it off in the first place. The smart part of your brain is telling you, "Put it off. Go to the zoo! Maybe a baboon will fall on you and you'll never have to do the task." This is known as the voice of reason. The Voice of Mom* is usually speaking in your other ear, saying, "Don't you feel *terrible*? Aren't you *ashamed*?" So if you're the kind of person who

* Long into adulthood, the Voice of Mom retains control over most of the channels in your brain, sort of like state radio in the Soviet Union. *Things Dad Said Once* get aired once a week in a regular time slot, sort of like *Prairie Home Companion.*

perversely enjoys being bad and wicked, you have a veritable symphony of neurological impulses going on in your brain.

Let's say people have told you, "It's better to make the *wrong* decision than no decision at all." The people who brought you Suez, the Little Bighorn, and the Charge of the Light Brigade are the ones saying this to you. No one knows how these people got airtime to be Voices in Your Head.

The reason the Voices in Your Head want so much for you to finish something is that the human organism longs for something called "closure" or "completion." The human organism cannot tolerate loose ends. This is why we buy products like "furniture finish" and "finishing rinse" for the hair, and Pearl Drops Tooth Polish for the dental work.

But when we think about it, not much in the natural world is ever truly completed. No one ever finished Paris or Istanbul. Schubert never finished his *Eighth Symphony*. (He didn't really die while writing it. That's just what they tell you. It was a nice day. He went to the dog track. He cleaned up in the Trifecta.)

A lot of people ask, "Am I a wicked person, just because I put hard things off?" And the answer is "Yes, you are a wicked person, but you are also an *intelligent* person."

If you wait long enough before doing something you will usually find that you had no reason to do it in the first place. The day the *Hindenburg* crashed, no one ever noticed how many people were late for work in Lakehurst, New Jersey.

THE NEW WORRY-ELITE

When nobody had any money, everybody naturally worried a great deal about *getting* some; but getting some money is a picnic-like experience compared with the effort people put into *keeping* some.

"Job satisfaction" used to be related to shallow goals like promotions, or salary, or the location of one's vacation home. But none of those things is really an indicator of how much you're really putting into holding on to that crazy green stuff. None of this is *body-and-soul, blood-and-guts* material. Only the number of stress disorders you've recently gotten medical attention for tells the true story.

Possibly you have heard two upwardly mobile professionals indulging in an increasingly popular diversion called "stress-disorder poker."

"Still being treated for that *hyperventilation* problem, Charley?"

"Nahh. That turned into *insomnia* and *sleepwalking* a long time ago. I've been getting *shingles* and *bleeding ulcers* on a regular basis, though, with a touch of *adult comedogenic acne,* and I'm fifty-six."

"Well, I'll raise you. I've had *hemorrhoids* and *spastic colitis* since Friday."

"Well, I'll see you the *spastic colitis,* and throw in *eczema* and *seborrhea,* and you probably didn't know about my *cocaine habit* and my *wife abuse. . . .*"

And so it goes.

It is a frightening thought that cumulative stress is beginning to inexorably alter the brain chemistry of those who are steering The Mighty Ship of the American Economy.

A LEADERSHIP CRISIS

We all know that every year, thousands of American children are lost in our National Parks because they lack the skills to abide in the wilderness. (They can no longer rub two sticks to make a fire, or suck venom from a snakebite.) But more chilling than this are the unpublished figures on *business executives* who sink without a trace in the nation's INDUSTRIAL PARKS.

In suburban areas of New York's Westchester County, California's Silicon Valley, and Boston's Route 128, "Industrial Parks" have become so devoid of identifying signs that busy executives can get lost in them for days, causing anguish to their family and friends. Stories abound of the

Texaco executive who accidentally wandered into IBM and for eight days dictated memos, attended board meetings, and used the Executive Men's Room, while Texaco security officers searched for him frantically on the beautifully landscaped corporate grounds of Texaco.

These stories, of course, speak for themselves, and represent tough realities that many Americans have to face.

GOOD NEWS AND BAD NEWS

This is why the mandatory taking of "vacation time" is starting to be *strictly enforced* by authorized agents, who are combing all workplaces in search of recalcitrant executives hiding under desks, in washrooms, and behind potted rubber trees.

Most executives know only too well what they are bargaining for when they sign on for a week of fun-in-the-sun; or two weeks, or even worse. Enforced indolence. Pop-it-bead commerce. And worse.

All civilized men dread the moment when they will be attending a performance of Festive Ethnic Dancing (in some foolish-but-happy tropical paradise) and will suddenly be GAILY WHISKED UP ONTO THE STAGE AND FORCED TO WHIRL ABOUT IN ANTIC MERRIMENT. Often while wearing suspect floral decorations, leis, muu-muus, sarongs, dhotis . . .

Consular officials are usually powerless to protect American Nationals when attacks by native folk dancers strike. Usually the native dancers' grasp of English is feeble, but their grip on one's extremities is ferocious.

!!!!!Investment counselors are asked to loosen or even remove their neckties, the better to gyrate their necks and collarbones.

!!!!!Grandmothers of twelve are forced to swivel their hips in the heathenish hula-hula.

!!!!!People in overly small stretch leisurewear are hauled up and applauded for having no shame whatsoever.

!!!!!People who refuse to dance are forbidden further access to Mai-Tais, Piña Coladas, and other hitherto free booty of the islands.

Forced participation in folk dancing is not the end of the story. Several weeks after the incident, and the humiliation, have worn off, one's boss often receives a thick envelope in the mail, postmarked "SAMOA" or "PORT-AU-PRINCE," and inside this envelope are photographs.

Several Third World countries base up to a fifth of their revenue on payoffs from top-level executives who wore *a lei too many* on that last vacation.

The saddest victims of all are the ones who were not quite pie-faced enough to have forgotten all the sordid details the morning after.

ONE WAY OF LOOKING AT THE WHOLE THING

It would be an amusing experiment if, *just for argument's sake,* we learned (don't go crazy when you read this, now—this is just a little "kind-of-offbeat" idea) to "lower our economic expectations," the way *U.S. News & World Report* keeps threatening every year that we may have to do.

Some young people at a high level of success undeniably have a hard time coping with the "lag time" between wanting something and getting it. It can be as short a time as fifteen seconds, or as long as six to eight weeks, for home delivery.

Something as simple as buying a "dream house," for example, results in unconscionable amounts of waiting and finagling—*finding* a real estate agent, *scouting out* desirable townships, *investigating* school systems and water quality and property taxes and so on . . .

Many of us have our dream house *already* picked out, only to hear the vexing news that *"someone is already living there."*

This is why many petulant workaholics are already lobbying to enact the "Instant Gratification Law." ("Insta-Grat" is popular usage. "Instant Gratification" takes too long to say.)

Under the Insta-Grat Law, you will be able to simply walk into a house and say to the owner, "I WANT TO LIVE HERE. TAKE OFF."

This is not a very kind attitude to have about life, you know. Some people, no matter how terrific a "decorator" office they may possess, are never too old to be spanked.

Menace in the Home

THE dangers that threaten us in the home are all-too-often unseen: radon gas, burning plastics, destructive ions, even noise pollution—the deadly "white noise" that issues from the neighbors' television sets. . . . And just as we can suffer from all kinds of pollutant smells and sounds, we can also suffer from "white sight"—the sight of aggressively unattractive neighbors who pollute our field of vision; and you cannot buy one of those smoke-sucking devices to make them go away.

Home has never been a proven sanctuary from terror, or the Red Cross would not continue religiously to remind us that 750,000 Americans a year die in common household accidents. They are burned by kitchen fires, garroted by defective clotheslines and Christmas tinsel, felled by roof beams; every year hundreds of Americans bring electric appliances and light bulbs into the bathtub and Professional Muggers find them there and stab them; every year millions of us accidentally remove our fingerprints with carrot scrapers, and become *unidentifiable,* and the FBI is forced to auction off our personal effects.

The psychic toll of menace-in-the-home has been enormous. Most people have, at least fifteen times in the past year, failed utterly at prying free the contents of "easy-open" containers, and most often, the directions have failed to warn us that *we never should have tried this sort of thing at home.* Even graduates of the Harvard Institute of Easy-Open Containers have to read lengthy textbooks day and night to keep the sum of their knowledge up-to-date. And most likely, you have been attempting to do this sort of thing in front of *impressionable youngsters.*

The statistics pouring in are far from reassuring:

- A growing number of people are secretly and desperately afraid of their Cuisinarts—not only in an assembled state, but lying in disarray on the counter; what is logically going to stop all those powerful blades from whirling outward and turning our arms into Cottage Fries?
- All of us are probably familiar with RUMP ROASTS THAT KILL. We know that if we essay to "oven-broil" any red meats according to the "butcher's directions," they will automatically and repeatedly set off our "smoke detectors" (which are automatically programmed to go off *on any random occasion*). Until the point when we say, "Enough!" and disconnect the things. And this will, of course, be precisely the night before Little Trixie will decide to play "Pyre on the Ganges" in the room where you stacked all your old newspapers and oil-soaked rags.
- Fear of telephone-answering machines is enjoying a grim renascence. A lot of people are aware that there are certain "rogue" answering-machine tapes under the influence of powerful underworld forces which we are not even aware of until we "accidentally" play the tapes backwards (much as we did with certain cuts of *Magical Mystery Tour* back in the sixties, when we realized Paul was wearing a number of serious Buddhist bad-luck and death symbols). Several cuts that have come up from the Already-Dead include "I am the egg man, you are the egg man, I killed Veronica at the sound of the tone."

Violence among household appliances reached, perhaps, an apex in the sixties, when washing machines felt a constant need to leap out at one's pets during the "spin" cycle, inducing coronary arrest, and worse.

And then automatic ice-making machines reached their ascendancy. Controlled by forces few of us wanted to understand, day and night they emitted trayfuls of niblet-sized H_2O. Long after we had a need for *any more ice,* we would lie awake and hear the plop-plop-plop in the freezer, the unmistakable whir of a higher intelligence reasoning, "Who knows? The entire population of Canada could show up some evening needing cold drinks. But then again, they may not. . . . But then again . . ."

"Please, God, NO MORE ICE!" we screamed into the void; and we dreamed of a kitchen worse than any Nuclear Winter, peopled by Killer Eskimos; children turned to Slush Puppies before our eyes.

The day we finally pulled the plug, and went back to standard metal ice-cube trays, many Americans wept.

THE MICRO-ISSUES

As children we grow up to quickly realize that most of the most pernicious dangers in the home are much too tiny to be seen with the naked eye—and that we must therefore assume that they are *always* present, *never* accounted for, and *eternally* lying in wait for the unwary, the foolish, the careless, and the unclean. (Most eleven-year-olds know, for example, that if you EVER EAT FROM A SPOON THAT ONCE TOUCHED CAT FOOD, you will die. And usually slowly, and in agony.) You will also die fairly instantly if you ever touch:

- The bottom part of the kitchen-sink drain
- Dead flies
- Libby's creamed corn
- The rubber part of a toilet plunger
- Someone else's Kleenex
- Most things under the porch

The most important function that your grandmother served in your life was to tell you about all the invisible things that could kill you *outside* the home, where you were powerless to do anything about them.

For example, during the building of America's Interstate Highway System, many exotic and serious diseases traveled upwards through the earth's crust from places like Indonesia and Borneo, AND YOU CAN STILL CATCH MOST OF THESE DISEASES FROM THE TOILET SEATS IN THE REST ROOMS ON THE PENNSYLVANIA TURNPIKE. (This is the reason that "sanitary" hot-air hand dryers were invented.)

As adults, however, within the coziness of our own four walls, we are all-too-clearly left to our own devices.

THE MACRO-ISSUES

How many of us are loath to confess to any belief in the "supernatural," and yet feel powerless in the face of daily, incontestable evidence that many standard household objects *in fact have lives of their own*! We cannot actually prove it, but sandwich bags, bent safety pins, and *pens that no longer write* have the terrifying ability to move and even *reproduce at will*—just as socks, needles, and house keys have the ability to spontaneously degenerate and disappear at random intervals. (Coat hangers, like lobsters, are thought to be carnivorous, and will literally consume their fellows when confined to a small space.)

And what we find in our mailboxes is yet more terrifying than the mind can conceive . . .

Perhaps you, too, are on the regular, computerized mailing list to receive THIRD-CLASS MAIL FROM THE DEVIL.

Probably you have suspected it for years, for Satan himself is crafty and oblique in his wooing:

WATCH THIS SPACE FOR INFORMATION ABOUT UPCOMING TAX-DEDUCTIBLE TRIPS TO PUERTO RICO AND ATLANTIC CITY, he tells you.

YOU MAY ALREADY BE A WINNER, he tells you.

FROZEN PUMPKIN PIES, $1.15, he tells you. SAVINGS THROUGHOUT THE STORE. (And often worse).

The DEVIL never rests when he can possibly make you a deal on a condo or a grocery item.

Yes, there are times when we feel like strangers in our own homes. Utility repairmen scorn us; our appliances foment massive discord; and so many of us say, "But at least I can turn to my PETS for comfort."

THE RISING TIDE: PET TERRORISM IN AMERICA

See which of these all-too-common scenes are familiar to you:

- You wake up in the morning and hear your cat quietly throwing up in the next room, so you get out of bed and find a rag, but the cat is actually sitting smiling in front of the TV set, and you search the house in vain for evidence of the gastrointestinal misdemeanor.
- Your cat runs out into the yard and "hides" when you are about to leave on vacation, and when you come back from vacation your cat will be sitting in the crawl space under the house, *either* in good health, *or* on the verge of decomposition (so that you will have to pay $580 to have the house professionally fumigated). You can only *guess.*
- Your dog makes it clear through example that he will *only* tear up the living-room when you are not at home; asleep; in the hospital; visiting "others"; or worse.

Pets, much like all Middle Eastern religious fanatics, are never less than masterful in their use of "inexorably implied violence," and it is only then that they give you their LIST OF DEMANDS. (Have you negotiated with a cat lately? They are not NEGOTIABLE DEMANDS.) Pets want *more quality time to work on improved sleeping positions*; they want *better-quality plastic dishes*; they want you to *turn out the lights more often*, so that they can chase INVISIBLE BOOGEYMEN in the dark.

The continued desire of pets to Come into the House is matched only by their unquenchable passion for Going Back out of the House, followed almost immediately by the bounding, pressing need to Come Back into the House, followed by an overthrusting, insatiable longing to Go Back out of the House Again, and this eternal, unalterable pattern repeats itself daily, weekly, and monthly.

(We have chosen to discuss pets pretty-much-interchangeably here, since the only meaningful difference between pets is the *part of their body* they use to destroy your home and furniture when you have offended them: dogs use teeth and tails; cats use claws and switchblades.)

Many of us sit around wondering, "What do animals *really* think about?" and "What would animals say to us if they could talk?"

Pets want us to wonder these things, you understand. They want us to devote large segments of our days to wondering *whether they are getting enough out of life.* They hunker down with beseeching eyes, in the manner of Al Jolson singing "Mammy," and we experience new frontiers of inadequacy.

Those of us who do not allow ourselves to be ruled by our pets have reached a new plateau in human development. Pets have a number of things to recommend them, after all: we do not have to dress for dogs, or explain current events to them; and despite what people tell you, *cats cannot really understand standard American English.* But pets can be "victims," too: the world is changing rapidly, and stories are coming in of Good Pets Gone Bad, hardened and toughened by suburban existence.

- Many upscale cats suffer from the serious eating disorder of CAT BULIMIA, in which they will gorge themselves on grass from the backyard, then force themselves to vomit on your husband's cashmere sweater—all this just to stay just as svelte and trim as the Abyssinian next door.
- Doggies trained to fetch have developed SEVERE PERSONALITY DISORDERS when their owners have thoughtlessly purchased automatic tennis-ball-serving machines—and left them running for IRRESPONSIBLE INTERVALS. At this writing, a wire-haired terrier named Pinky has been involved in the same game of "fetch" for 12½ years. (And that's almost a century in *human* years.)
- CAT TOY ADDICTION reaches shocking new levels every year. All-too-often, the owner prematurely discards the "toy," and the cat goes through excruciating withdrawal, often peddling her body on the street TO BUY MORE YARN TOYS.
- CATS LIVE IN FEAR that because of their anthropomorphic possibilities, they will be seized and forced to pose in nurse's uniforms and black lace panties on the fronts of popular greeting cards. Known as "kitty porn," this is a burgeoning industry that takes in mil-

lions each year, and the kittycats involved are usually remunerated with little more than a pat on the neck and year's supply of felt mousies to Have Their Way With.

ONE LAST TERROR

At least even the most disturbed, unpardonable pets are mortal creatures; whereas it is a sad and true fact that unwanted, unsightly *house plants* are *not mortal.*

Always remember that you could, in theory, shoot an ugly or obstreperous pet to death, but there is no way to rid yourself of ugly house plants—especially those presented to you as gifts—since they will not die under any conditions. Starvation and poisoning do not work. Leave them out on the road under the wheels of cars, and some Good Samaritan will just deliver them back to your doorstep with a kindly, heartfelt note attached.

You will feel like Hitler for having done this. The motto of all house plants is "They Also Scoff, Who Only Sit and Vegetate."

Count your blessings here. Try to fill your home only with vertebrates.

The Edibles Complex

Ask any foreigner, "Do you eat to live, or do you live to eat?" and he would not answer you because he would be too busy chewing.

Living to eat has always been a suspect philosophy in America. ("Of *course* Rome wasn't built in a day," we are fond of saying. "They were always eating *lunch.* Maybe if they'd asked *us* to do it, things would have worked out *different.*") Americans have always been rightly credited with the invention of "fast food"; but our even *greater* world contribution of extremely *bad* food, such as BacOs, diet pudding, and individually wrapped cheese slices, has always gone unlauded and unappreciated.

But things are changing fast. Boatloads of "sophisticated," "global" foods are arriving on our shores so rapidly, we cannot stop them even with space-age "early detection" equipment.

This is not just a case of a *tostada* here, a *lutefisk* there; a *tempura* here, a *prosciutto* there—this is a culinary revolution in a nation that not so long ago thought that Communists were responsible for the invention of hearty brown mustard. (And they *were*, too: Just ask for a hot dog in the Midwest now, and *see* whether they give you *regular* French's anymore. And after that, they'll say, "How about some *borscht* with that?" and start to sing you the "Internationale.")

Even something as basic as *bread* is not immune from this sort of stylistic tampering. An unprecedented number of foreign breads are finding their way into our diets, most notably *croissants,* Irish soda bread, and Middle Eastern pita pockets—the BREAKFAST OF TERRORISTS, ladies and gentlemen! Before long, little kids will be saying, "None of that limp-wristed Wonder Bread, Mom! I intend to grow up and *never shave*!"

Naturally, there has been talk of establishing a "Food Border Patrol," to keep the American food intact and the suspicious food out—but how could you even keep such an arm of the government honest? They would be awash in bribes of *julienned* vegetables and green tea ice cream and white chocolate and *picante* sauce.

GNAWING ON THE UNKNOWABLE

Of course, America has lived through food crises before, and emerged stronger and wiser from them.

- Years ago, for example, Americans assimilated "pimentos" into their diet, even though no one has ever had any idea what "pimentos" *are,* and no one wants to admit that they *still do not know.* Are there pimento forests? Do pimentos grow underground? Do they use laser technology to get them inside of olives? Are pimentos taken more seriously in other countries than they are here? (Do they say, "Eat your pimentos, Ladislas, and you'll grow up big and strong"?)

  There are two kinds of Americans functioning today: those who are "prisoners" of pimentos, and rush out to the 24-hour Pathmark *every time* they see them on a recipe; and those who say, "No way. *Pimentos shall not cramp my lifestyle,* thanks a bunch." They dare their dinner guests to notice the absence of pimentos in their dinner fare.
- Every year, thousands of innocent Americans order ice cream cones with "Jimmies" sprinkled on top, and yet no one ever bothers to ask, "What is the chemical content of a 'Jimmy,' please?" This is innocence beyond the pale, when you stop to consider that every year, thousands of members of the Teamsters Union disappear without a trace, and most of them are named "Jimmy."
- A few years ago, the rumor surfaced that McDonald's

was putting kangaroo meat in its Big Macs (and several McDonald's chief executives had to hastily revise memos in which they claimed to be "hopping mad" about the accusation). And even though these rumors have been laid to rest, don't you tend to wonder about the contents of "Skippy" peanut butter?

- *Lime Jell-O tampering* in bus-station cafeterias was a serious health hazard in the late fifties and early sixties. Dessert material served in bus stations has almost always been the green kind, as a general rule of thumb, because then you could look at it and say, "Is this the *natural hue* of this foodstuff?" and the ladies in the hairnets who served it could look at you as if you were a life form from another dimension.

  There was also a serious conspiracy among mothers and bus stations and the *Ladies' Home Journal* in the early sixties to insert grated *carrots* into perfectly harmless Jell-O, so that it would become "Rainbow Jell-O Salad," and worse. If God had meant for *vegetable matter* to go into pure Jell-O, he would have let us know in some intelligible way.
- *Botulism* was a fairly rampant food-poisoning craze of the sixties. People trembled at the thought of "the tuna that kills"—*canned goods on the march* to destroy mankind. It was a dramatic kind of death that hit you before you even reached for the Miracle Whip; nine times out of ten, rigor mortis set in so fast, they had to bury you with the can opener in your hand. "Watch out for dents and pinholes," they told you. "Never eat out of a can of Campbell's soup that is larger than a football! Never eat out of a can that has a skull and crossbones on the label!"
- *"Food biography"* has probably been the most frightening food trend of the early eighties—which is to say that you used to be able to go to a restaurant and see "steak" and "peas" (or, at the very worst, "*garden-fresh* peas") on a menu; but then the steak started getting "biodynamically nutrified," and it wasn't long before the steak was "nurtured on the shores of Lake Morehouse in the Canadian Laurentians in a stress-free environment, and slaughtered humanely by the 'Singing' cow-slaughterers

of the Abattoir Ste.-Duglère, Natchez, Maine," and you could not leave the restaurant without sobbing uncontrollably into a handkerchief.

AN IMPORTANT HISTORY OF FOOD

Maybe the thought has crossed *your* mind, while driving in your car or waiting in line at an out-of-service cash machine, or otherwise usefully occupied:

HOW DID ANCIENT PEOPLE DECIDE WHAT YOU COULD EAT AND WHAT YOU COULDN'T?

Everyone must have made some important mistakes along the way. Tomatoes were long thought to be poison until a brave Frenchman visiting Padua, Italy, ate a tomato on the steps of the town hall, and *did not perish* in any noticeable way. "Coffee" is a harder thing to figure out. Did someone in South America say, "Let's boil some roasted beans in water, and then *sit up all night* twitching a lot and talking in very rapid, irritated voices?"

Which inevitably leads you to "Who figured out cottage cheese?" Which leads you to "Who figured out *head* cheese?"

We know that the idea of "agriculture" began somewhere in Mesopotamia in the late Bronze Age, when everyone was tired of consuming bronze three meals a day, so they all went outside to see what was growing in the dirt. *"There is many vitamins in this dirt,"* said many forward-thinking Bronze Age people; so certain selected "designated eaters" experimented with eating the dirt. Then they experimented with broccoli. Somewhere in the next 355,000 years or so, someone invented Libby's creamed corn niblets, although no one has any explanation as to why.

The evolution of meat-eating was a lot more touch-and-go. Early cave people perfected the art of hunting in about 100,000 B.C. and wasted a number of years experimenting with eating the fur of animals and *wearing* the meat; but the meat was difficult to divide into sizes, and several female "cave personnel" (as they insisted on being called) objected to wearing "one-size-fits-all" meat, so the idea was abandoned. Eventually, a meat-and-anthracite casserole was deemed acceptable by a number of people, and the idea of carnivorousness really caught on.

In this country, the ambivalence about eating animal body parts particularly has reached a fairly frenzied level. Most of us, as young children, perfected the "Hemingway," or "matador" tactic of attacking liver—whereby we did not so much eat it, as make *passes* at it. ("*Olé,* Timmy; now eat the damn thing.") It became a sort of ceremonial mortal combat. (The liver usually won. If you visit your old neighborhood of twenty years ago, your house will have turned into condo units, but the liver will still be there behind the étàgere where you hid it, having a half-life comparable to those of uranium and carbon compounds.)

It is a transcendent irony, then, that most of the Completely Gross Foods you wisely and knowledgeably barfed up as a youngster are now described in shimmering terms on the pages of *The New York Times Cookbook.* What, pray tell, are these *terrines* and *pâtes,* if not plain old LIVER, all tricked out with a fancy *accent aigu* at the end?

FOOD AND EMOTIONAL LIFE

Yes, it would be vulgar to say that we are a nation which lives to eat, but no one could dispute that we are a nation which lives to *discuss* eating. In fact, if someone doesn't uncover a new, more pernicious food "additive" or "eating disorder" soon, the staff of the *Phil Donahue Show* may have to devise one, or offer a cash reward.

It fascinates us that there are "problem" foods, and, ergo, "solution" foods. Foods which will lay us low, and foods which will guarantee that we be eulogized as "winners." (The book *Eat to Get Married,* though not yet written, has a pre-earned spot on the *New York Times* best-seller list.)

Some say that we humans feel a sort of massive institutionalized guilt over the way we've misbehaved ourselves en route to the top of the food chain. We did a lot of honking and pushing and shoving on our way past the minor vertebrates and legumes and mollusks and gastropods, which has made us, in some vague way, highly apologetic to Baser Life Forms in general.

It could have worked out differently. If cows ate people, they probably wouldn't name us awful things like "Bossy," and make us stand around staring glazedly at the same hunk of turf all day. Maybe cows would even let us stand up and stretch or take in a movie occasionally.

Only cows know for sure, and they're not telling.

Modern Technology: Threat or Hazard?

It is difficult to know, on any given day of any given week, whether it is considered more hip and fashionable to be *for* technology, or to be *against* it. The minute you say "I was 'resistant' to my automatic garage-door opener at first," everybody looks at you curiously and says, "We're doing ours *manually* these days. We think it's important for the children to see."

There is, of course, the obvious argument that due to "progress" our five senses are becoming creaky and underutilized. For centuries, land mammals have relied for survival on their sense of *scent,* for example—sniffing out predators, following spoors, processing wind-borne olfactory warnings. Man, being descended from the first mammal to develop the opposable thumb, is also the first to have invented antiperspirant. Some say the discovery has led inevitably to confusion, madness, and crime.

There are others who say that it doesn't matter that technology has left us feeling that "we hardly know whether we're coming or going"; the point is that we always know how *fast,* and at what *temperature,* thanks to the magic of digital readouts.

TECHNOLOGICAL AMBIVALENCE ON THE MARCH

Now that Serious Technology abounds in the average home, myths have inevitably circulated about the harm it can do.

- It's commonly believed, for example, that if you push the wrong sequence of buttons on your VCR, you can get sucked into another dimension—a dimension of sight and sound, but not of mind and body. (It's possible to get back out of this dimension by pushing the same buttons from *inside* your VCR, but you have to remember to do it backwards and inside out.)
- Home-security professionals claim that their systems have become so sophisticated that they can monitor the brain waves of nearby burglars who are even *thinking* of knocking over your home on any given night.

  This is not entirely true. Perhaps the most brilliant and frightening antiburglar technology now available is the timer-controlled system that can turn on your lights, stereo, and noise-making appliances *regardless of whether you are home or not.* Which leaves you with the depressing knowledge that your house is having more fun when you are not around, and probably wishes you would stay away permanently.
- Even the simple telephone packs its share of portent. Many people are reluctant to answer their home phones these days because they are "deeply afraid," or, worse, have reason to believe it is "someone calling." At least before telephones were invented, they could just say to their butlers, "Inform Mr. Fortescue that I am not at home, Charles."

Alexander Graham Bell realized late in life what a monster he had created in the telephone, so he spent the latter part of his life perfecting "the hot shower" so that he would always be unavailable to answer it.

TECHNOLOGY AS YOUR FRIEND

This is just one side of the story, of course.

Imagine, for a moment, a world *without* "local shopping malls."

Who would have guessed a thousand years ago that you could go shopping even on a rainy, sleety day without wetting your feet or damaging your coif, because you would be in a place where *there isn't any weather*?

The way in which they've managed not to have any weather in shopping malls is that they've found a way to completely and safely remove *all the actual air*. There is some stuff in malls that feels like oxygen, but it is in truth a state-of-the-art industrial-strength *oxygen substitute,* certified on lab rats to be nontoxic, and undetectable to the naked eye.

All the doors in shopping malls have little atriums where you can decompress, so that when you exit, the actual oxygen in the parking lot won't kill you. What you've been breathing, mostly, is other people's *safely processed used breath*: the airborne detritus, say, of the lungs of cheerleaders. It's probably one of those realities of science that the less you know about it, the better.

(Lately, of course, there has been a great panic afoot that *there will not be enough malls for future generations* because we simply cannot construct them fast enough. But there is a hot line for Americans to call if they spot a single abandoned twine factory, warehouse, office building, or public school that has not yet been converted into a shopping mall.)

This is just *one* of the boons of modern technology.

If you were to gather a roomful of great scientists, ethnographers, futurists, and sociobiologists and ask them "What are the four greatest things the technological revolution has brought us?" they would almost be compelled to answer TV sets, personal computers, air travel, and Professionally Dry Clean Only "miracle" fabrics, in roughly that order.

"WHEN DO YOU WANT IT BY?"

We tend to pooh-pooh the importance of quality dry cleaning in our professional lives, but where would we all be if we were out on our lunch hours beating our Pierre Cardin suits on rocks?

We had to reach a highly industrialized state in order for "dry-clean only" or "all-white" clothing to even be invented —since "dry-clean only" clothing eventually costs you about $9,860 more than you actually paid for it; and "all-white" clothing only remains "all-white" on the Pope, other people, and, occasionally, Cheryl Tiegs.

(All-white clothing is known to have some very unusual properties indeed. While you are looking at it in the store, it rarely has any visible spots or markings on it; but over a short period of time, spots frequently develop *on their own,* without any assistance from you—very much like undeveloped Polaroid film. A man once brought home the wrong all-white clothing and found that it eventually developed a full-color print of the Edgar Rawlins family of Smithtown, L.I. Also two attractive wallet-size photos, suitable for framing.)

Dry-cleaning science is awesome in its scope and power. We try not to think about what happens to our navy blue blazer when it disappears "behind the curtains" at a dry-cleaning establishment; just as we try not to think about the size of the universe, or what happened to Michael Rockefeller when he disappeared among the headhunters of New Guinea. We don't want to know how many vats of contraband ocher chemicals are back there foaming passionately (or how many perspiring aliens in bamboo cages, living on scorpions and table scraps)—as long as they get the cat hair out by Wednesday.

We give our dry cleaners infinite authority in our lives. The dry cleaner *always takes down your address* (Ever wonder about this? What is he going to do? Send you a chain letter?) and says, "When do you want it by?" (This is a little "joke" of his. It is sort of like people in the Ukraine thinking they have a choice on election day between the Communist Party and the Mouseketeers.)

Despite all the above, most dry cleaning—even awesomely *bad* dry cleaening—is rarely, if ever, a direct threat to one's life and personal well-being.

GETTING AIRBORNE

Every year since Kitty Hawk, thousands of Americans have earnestly enrolled in sessions designed to "cure" them of their fear of aviation.

It is a distinctly modern concept: that people who have a normal, biologically intact WILL TO LIVE should need, in some way, to be "cured."

Nobody ever talks about sending pilots to seminars to rid them of the notion that they can take a 150-ton hunk of aluminum with 220 humans (and their dependents) aboard *and lift it clear off the ground—for hours at a time.*

Clearly, this is a case where people with a SUSPECT, CAVALIER ATTITUDE toward all the natural laws of the universe are being given the upper hand, and nobody really knows who started this alarming precedent, or why. Great minds like Isaac Newton, and others, labored for hundreds of years to popularize the invention of gravity, so that most life forms (with the exception of birds and mosquitoes, who never interested anyone intelligent) would be on terra firma, and all present and accounted for.

In order to keep millions of (paying) individuals airborne, day after day, the aviation industry has had to come up with ingenious techniques to convince people they are doing something "safe," "wholesome," "economical," and even "fun."

1) *"What do I know?"*

From the very first moments of a commercial flight, airlines try to subtly convince people that everything they know about the universe, and specifically, reality, is faulty. They serve you beverages out of teeny-tiny bottles that look like relics of *Thumbelina's Alcoholic Playhouse.* They have men and women waiting on you who look exactly like "real" people, only they smile and say "Oops" every time the aircraft hits an air pocket large enough to send you to certain, screaming, flesh-charring death. These "flight attendants" answer your most urgent questions with carefully crafted masterpieces of illogic: When you start to notice a burning smell immediately after takeoff, and you ask the attendant what it is, he or she just says, "Oh, that's probably lunch." And when you say, "Really? What are we getting for lunch?" they say, "Cold cuts."

These people would certainly be unidentifiable after any major in-flight disaster because, although they have four times as many teeth as you or anyone else, *you have to be a human being to have dental records.*

2) *They try to tell you that it helps to familiarize yourself with the "emergency exits."*

We all know that in the "unlikely event" of a tragedy, everyone in a burning aircraft stands politely in line and says, "After you, Old Thing. Frightful bother being cremated like this, what? How about those Cubs?"

It was rumored for a while that sitting in the rear, or "smoking," section of an aircraft was "safer." In 1980, 85 percent of people who survived plane crashes did so because they were declared "smokers." Within five years, all these people had died of emphysema or heart disease.

3) *"The best thing to do is relax and enjoy the flight."*

In 1978, the FAA published a set of findings stating that there were three major factors at work in propelling an aircraft off the ground and keeping it aloft: functional design, airspeed, and massive group prayer. Sure, on any given flight there are passengers strolling the aisles and chatting and reading 1984 issues of *Business Week*; but the real, unsung heroes of any flight are the *chanting* passengers —the ones have devoted themselves to the correct mantra and have taken upon themselves the survival of every man, woman, and child aboard that particular DC-10.

These brave people refuse sedation, or visits to the rest room, or comfy pillows (which could lead to *dozing off*), or idle conversation about oil prices, hem lengths, or things to do in Munich. Anything that affects these people's concentration affects the entire outcome of the flight: Life or Death; Feast or Famine; Happy Landing or Grisly Statistic!

Airline spokesmen are often quoted as saying that it is the *pilots* who are responsible, but commercial pilots are carefully taught to believe that what they are seeing out their windows is a *giant video flight simulator.* If they really believed that they were leaving the ground in giant aluminum tubes with peanuts and living passengers and vacuum toilets, do you honestly think they could hold on to their sanity for more than a week?

THIS JUST IN . . .

High technology has brought us television, as no one has to tell us, and most specifically, the galvanizing phenomenon of "Action News." Late-breaking news, recently breaking news, currently breaking news, news that is holding its breath just waiting to erupt.

Nowadays on "Action News," we are treated to the sight of professional women named "Janee" and "Rowlanda" (professional local newswomen are never named anything normal. They need names that are—*you* know—*newsy*), and "Janee" or "Rowlanda" is standing in front of a large sinkhole. (Large urban sinkholes are always considered "Action" news—although you sort of wish the sinkhole would do something to rate all that airtime, like sing a little tune or swallow up a tour bus.)

"Janee" or "Rowlanda" always tells you that the "situation is developing," or that she is "*on top of* a developing situation." (Could this be the terminology these women use at home in describing their sex lives?) Ideally somebody is holding somebody hostage, or somebody with a lot of telegenic hostility is negotiating a contract, or terrorists are chasing the floats of the Macy's Thanksgiving Day Parade with the world's largest pointed instrument.

A lot of people are beginning to despair of living in areas where there is a great deal of "Action News." At one point people in New York and Detroit were evacuating these areas in record numbers and going to live in Idaho and Nevada and the New Mexico desert, but now they have "Action News" in those places too.

Recently, in Palm Springs, California, they experimented by broadcasting an edition of "Passive News" on morning drive-time radio, but a number of people fell asleep at the wheel and ended up in ditches along a thirteen-mile stretch of highway.

In the end, they had to send in a minicam and Monitor the Situation as It Developed.

CHIP WARS

Home computers are, of course, the most difficult thing to know nowadays whether to be "for" or "against."

On the one hand, you envy all those people who are seriously "into" their computers—the ones who tie up your phone lines, yodeling, "Give it a chance, you cranky old dinosaur! You're *extinct,* you're *linear,* you're *Stone Age City*!" And they tell you they could no longer so much as "spell their name" without their "PC" anymore.

It is very important to humbly nod to *the superior intellect* of people like this; it is very immature of you to secretly wish that sooner or later a massive sunspot will knock out every functioning power source on the planet, making you, by default, the most literate, powerful person on earth.

Personally, you are wary of any form of technology that is called a "processor"—whether what it "processes" is words, foods, block diagrams, or fish meal. If you are a maladroit or groggy author with a lot of gadgets, what is really to *stop* you from feeding your completed novel into the wrong "processor," and turning it into a *delicious cold soup*? *(Yes*—no messy cleanup, peels, pits, or cores; and also, no royalties and *no Donahue.)*

Perhaps you have heard the recent rumor, bruited about in every checkout line in America, that Home Computers are Controlled by Satan Himself, and that the display screen of a Macintosh 19-SA is in fact THE DEVIL'S WINDSHIELD. But it is much more likely that, if "by" anybody, home computers are controlled by the spirit of the kid who used to beat you up and steal your lunch money in fourth grade.

Lots of times when you type and print a document that looks pretty "letter quality" to *you,* the display screen will go into the "SNEER MODE," and flash at you:

DOCUMENT PRINTED

DOCUMENT CONTAINS "FORMATTING ERRORS."

GUESS WHICH "FORMATTING ERRORS" THEY WERE.

GIVE UP?

HA-HA-HA-HA-HA-HA

The thing that probably bothers you most about computers is that there are people out there who are not exactly Rhodes Scholars who know more about computers than you ever will. And when you get your computer home from the computer store, everyone tells you that there is nothing a seventh-grade graduate or other *low-grade feeb* could not easily figure out in moments.

Indeed, the User's Manual contains drawings of a winsome yellow birdie in a lion tamer's costume, blithely inserting diskettes into a-drives and b-drives, and disconnecting the coaxial cables from the connectors on their cluster adaptors. You see pastel horsies and kitties attaching graphics/matrix printers to their systems, and de-bugging their DOS diskettes and handling static-sensitive devices, and then settling down for a cool drink over the 9-pin signal connector on their color/graphics monitor adaptor.

The minute *you* bravely "boot in" your system, you smell something that reminds you of burning nylon hosiery, and when you attempt to issue a command to the system, you see something like "EXCUSE ME, MOI?" on the display screen, which does not exactly make you prickle with the righteous pride of ownership.

Many of us have already suspected that this is the case, but most word processors and videocassette recorders can *actually communicate with each other*; and they do it in a special encoded language, known as

OWNR IS A: ½ WIT

They beep each other messages like

DID YOU CATCH WHT OWNR WAS *WERING* TODAY? CUD YU *STAND* IT?

Occasionally, your VCR and your PC have microchip intercourse, and that electrical fume you smell afterwards is the two of them enjoying a cigarette.

Can You Be Friends with Your Brain?

WHAT do human beings, station wagons, and plutonium all have in common?

Under the right conditions, they are all capable of something *very* special in life known as a "breakdown."

"Breakdowns" don't happen to just *anyone,* although many of us brag nearly every day that we are "about" to have one—but then we fail to follow through because some kind of last-minute "emergency" comes up. (Failing to Follow Through with a Breakdown is an accepted form of false advertising in the wacky world of interpersonal communication.)

Throughout the millennia those of us "disposed to breakdown" (known as the "breakdown-friendly") have developed a unique approach to our daily problems, known as "repression." The "repressed" approach has led to people making some *very* interesting decisions behind the wheels of cars at 75 mph; but it has also made sex (not *intrinsically* a very interesting activity) one of the most universally fascinating subjects on earth.

An incipient breakdown can attack you just as easily sleeping or waking. Sometimes you can sit up in bed in the morning feeling perfectly fine, and then discover that you have bitten the leg off your end table, or awakened half the neighbors screaming, "MITZI MUST DIE!"

STRANGER-THAN-TRUTH BEDFELLOWS

Perhaps you'd like to play "guest shrink" for a minute, and work on the significance of the following all-too-common anxiety dreams:

You are having dinner in a restaurant with Dr. Henry ("the maneuver") Heimlich. You get a large bit of steak lodged in your throat and begin gagging and choking violently. Dr. Heimlich says, "Waiter, check, please."

You are on your usual commute over the Liberty Bridge into Pittsburgh, only the bridge has been replaced by a thin strand of hemp rope, and all the commuters are dressed like Indiana Jones and crossing the rope bridge hand-over-hand. You are wearing bedroom slippers.

You are climbing Mount Lassen with your eleventh-grade physics teacher and Broadway producer DAVID MERRICK. And when you look at the mountain, you realize that it is actually a giant stack of high school senior themes on "The Most Unforgettable Person I Have Ever Met." Mr. Merrick tells you that he would like you to turn these documents into a musical comedy. By Wednesday.

You are being stood up in front of a firing squad, and everyone you have ever met is seated in bleachers as an audience. Your mother is selling popcorn.

All these dreams fill you with a sense of futility and inadequacy. In fact, this is an area where PROFESSIONAL THERAPY can serve as "an anchor" in your life. Therapy can replace the nagging suspicion that you are inadequate with a sense of absolute certainty that you are.

A LIFE ON THE COUCH

It is ironic that no one ever *expects* to be in therapy for more than a few months. Therapy is sort of like going to a mechanic and saying you have a little rattle in the engine, and he says, "Fine, you can have the car next week." And you come back in a week and he has completely taken the car apart and all the pieces are lying on the floor of the garage.

"What good is my car in a million pieces?" you say to the mechanic, and he nods wisely and says, "Ah, but at least everything is out where you can *see it*."

A lot of people fear the "power" of the therapist, who can seemingly say some kind of "magic word," and your mind just suddenly flips open, like one of those improved new toothpaste dispensers.

But actually, there is nothing intrinsically harmful about "free association."

Say your sister "Bette Black" has always been your *bête noire,* so you spend a lot of time dreaming about black sheep causing a big fight in the backseat of a '64 Impala. After about five years of analysis, your therapist might point out that sheep rarely ride in the backseat of Chevrolet autos, and that your association is probably "symbolic" of something. You might say something along the lines of "Son-of-a-gun." Or even "Aha."

This is why therapy is a good idea if you intend to stay in it for about seventy-eight years, and you have an endless capacity for saying things like "I think I'm getting close to something, but I don't know what it is."

You will never find out what "it" is, but you will get closer and closer to "it" as therapy progresses.

YOUR BRAIN, MADE SIMPLE

In general, professional therapists do not like it very much if you go around reading psychology textbooks and interpreting the information you read all by yourself. Therapists are afraid that this practice will put "ideas in your head," and they feel that your head is a very bad place for ideas ever to be.

But since you are the only landlord specifically empowered to administrate the space between your ears, perhaps you should have a better idea of the tenants living up there.

The brain actually consists of three jolly components: the id, the ego, and the "Superego."

The Superego is the part of the brain that polices your activities, telling you you shouldn't slice the arms off kittens and sass your parents and steal from vending machines. (The id says, "What do you think you've got thin wrists for? Steal from vending machines! Make sure you get a Chunky bar!" The ego usually gets caught in the crossfire during exchanges like this and has to sit around a lot waiting things out; usually getting hungry.)

It is the Superego which endows us with the power to "feel guilty" about things. It is ironic that the U.S. Constitution grants us the right to life, liberty, and the pursuit of Quite a Lot of Fun. And yet our Pilgrim forefathers eschewed gratuitous amounts of fun (especially when there were rows to be hoed and turkeys to be plucked).

We are in a quandary because the Principles of Country & Western Music demand that we pursue fun in its many dimensions, particularly pickin' and grinnin' and other activities.

And we feel understandably torn between Fun and Non-Fun.

It is our Superego that usually stands in the Doorway to Fun and says, "I'm sorry. I don't see your name on the list here. . . ."

TRICKS OF THE BRAIN

Carl Jung went a little further in picking apart the brain in his ground-breaking work on "the human unconscious." Your "unconscious," you see, is always with you—the part of your brain you don't have access to and frequently don't want to know about. ("*That* brain! I've never seen it before in my life!") Think of it sort of as a movie version of your real life, only with much better dialogue. The showtimes only occur when you are asleep.

Members of primitive societies were able to transfer their "evil" unconscious thoughts into all sorts of inanimate or subhuman things, like trees, shrubbery, chickens, and hyenas. In modern society, only younger brothers fulfill this function. (As in *"Louis did it."*) If you were a Masai warrior, you could just say "A *chicken* did it," and not even get spanked. In cases like this, primitive people often had a better deal.

Freud believed greatly in the secret power of the unconscious. In his great book *Die Accidenten Existen Nicht,* he stated that there was no such thing as "common household accidents." "Little bitty accidents are always a message C.O.D. from the unconscious," Freud said, "so heads up and give a listen." When you "bite your tongue," are you not feeling remorse over some harsh words you spoke to a friend? When you "stumble" on the rug, are you not "tripping up" a desire to throttle a parent or child? When you hold a revolver against your temple and squeeze off six shots in rapid succession (as reported by a patient of Freud's who was rejected by the military because of ear trouble), are you not "blowing your brains out" in the hope of "dying immediately" and thus ending your misery?

UNDERSTANDING MODERN TERMS

Many of the findings of Freud and Jung have been debunked by "new-wave" mental-health professionals, who feel much more comfortable using terminology from a number of modern disciplines, such as nuclear physics, childrens' literature, cooking, and horticulture.

Probably the most important part of your modern personal-growth regimen is knowing whether or not you are "centered." And what kind of "center," you may ask, do you need?

It is helpful to think of it this way. There are two kinds of people: Avocado people and Twinkie people.

Twinkie people have a soft, cream-filled center. (Also, if you look closely, they have been getting smaller in recent years, which may be significant, and then again may not.)

Avocado people are smooth and rich on the outside and have a hard, firm inner core. An avocado is *centered.* Think of an avocado without its center and all you have is guacamole.

How do you know if *you* have a "center"?

- Do you listen constantly to the opinions of other people? Do you keep a notebook of the opinions of other people, just in case you get asked your opinion and you know in advance you aren't going to have one?
- Do you watch commercial endorsements by actors who play doctors on TV (and when the actor says, "I'm not a doctor, but an actor who plays a doctor on TV," do you say to yourself, "Well, what the hoo-ha? I'm going to buy that product *anyway.* He sure *looks* like a doctor"?).
- Do you buy sex manuals authored by people whose book-jacket photos clearly indicate they've never had sex in their lives?

If any of this applies to you, do not despair.

Being "centered" is only a word so far, not an actual *thing.* If it ever becomes a "thing," then you should worry.

GETTING NORMAL

Many people opt to leave therapy when they reach the age of adulthood (usually around thirty-eight), citing such reasons as "finding new resources of self-esteem," "learning to accept my true identity," and "running completely out of money."

At this point, the therapist counsels the patient on whether he or she is making the "right decision."

WELL, ARE *YOU?*

They say that one of the main points of therapy is to *get rid of your rage.* But a lot of people don't realize that their rage is much more interesting than they are.

If Frank Kafka had gone into therapy, for example, he would have become an accordionist and played at weddings. If W. A. Mozart had gone into therapy, he would have "symbolically separated" from his father, Leopold. If Mad King Ludwig of Bavaria had gone into therapy, he would have become Outpatient King Ludwig, and none of his castles would have been listed in *Europe on $20 a Day.*

Probably you can't help wondering what people did in the 5,000-odd years of human evolution before therapy was invented. What did people do when they had personality disorders, for example, in ancient Egypt?

Let's say there was a certain middle-class Joe in downtown Luxor who had a lot of problems: he was worshiping a particular cat who didn't return his affections, and then he lost his job down at the Papyrus Outlet, and then the River Nile flooded all over his new Prayer Carpets, and he was losing sleep imagining the pyramids were moving fifteen cubits west each day, and his mother was demanding and Tut-tutting him all the time, and he didn't know where to turn, because all the available oracles were booked up for the month. It wasn't as if there were some overeducated Egyptian with a goatee and a rented office who could charge him 50 pieces of gold an hour to free-associate. He had to figure out the answers *himself.*

Therapists cannot convincingly argue that their skills are the glue which is keeping Civilization as We Know It (in the absence of a truly effective United Nations) from falling apart at the seams.

At best, they can only argue that if everyone in therapy suddenly dropped out tomorrow—and everyone's extra $75-a-week suddenly went into mass circulation—then international trade would be unbalanced to such a degree that the New York Stock Exchange would have to close down for a week, giving the Soviet Union a chance to move in on every Western Alliance nation.

It is a thought that every one of us should conscientiously work to repress.

IV

The Good Stuff

Love and Romance

LOVE is categorically different from all other human belief systems, faiths, and forms of group hysteria.

Unlike "believing in" ghosts and flying saucers, for example, people seem to "believe in" love in inverse proportion to the degree to which they've been exposed to it.

And given a choice between a "roomful of ghosts" and a "roomful of ex-fiancés," most Respected Scientists would only pay good money to be included in the former.

Love is one of the most popular emotions of all time and yet it seems to be mishandled almost constantly.

The first principle that you as a would-be candidate should bear in mind is that:

REALITY STOPS HERE

It would be wonderful if the person we are presently in love with could actually be the same person we first fell in love with, but this is almost never the case. When we meet someone on a first date, we are not actually ourselves but rather life-sized replicas of ourselves, spouting all kinds of unique statements which may bear some passing resemblance to the truth, but which usually do not.

- "You're kidding! You love Estonian food *too*!"
- "On a beautiful summer day, I too love to spend the afternoon in a tomblike basement of the Chicago Art

Institute looking at Goya etchings of High Points of the Spanish Inquisition!"

- "I'm such an *all-night dancing fool, they don't call me Happy Legs for nothing*!"
- "Oh, darling, I too cannot wait to check out the pan-Islamic folk-dancing tour of the northern Indus Valley, rather than go to Disney World this year."

On a first date, we almost never hear our mother's voice coming out of our mouths, as per normal reality, but rather a new, exciting voice that, with meditation and prayer, could even be ours!

Love is actually a cleverly disguised "What if—?" proposition. What if gentlemen didn't really prefer blondes? What if love really were "blind"? What if I decided to behave like someone else entirely, and pulled the thing off for years at a time? And sometimes we get away with strategies like this; and very often, we don't.

DOES THIS MEAN THAT LOVE IS ACTUALLY DANGEROUS?

It is true that when you are deeply in love you become alarmingly out of touch with the simple functions that tend to get you through the day. (Viz. the song "I Didn't Know What Time It Was." It is a bad idea to call people's answering machines if such is the case with you, since this is the minimum information you are usually expected to be on top of.) People even lose their entire sense of propriety and syntax. George Gershwin went around saying alarming things like "Bess, You Is My Woman Now," which led almost inevitably to the strange logistics of "Love Lifts You Up Where You Belong."

Even if there were a known over-the-counter medication for the alarming physical side effects of True Love, most people would speed right past their local pharmacy, on one of the many well-traveled shortcuts to the Heartbreak Hotel.

THE ROOTS OF THE EMOTION: HOW YOU LEARN TO LOVE

The young infant loves only his mother and his Gumby and whoever feeds him. He has what is called an "oral fixation," which means he loves whatever he can fit into his mouth. This is why he has no teeth—so that there is room for him to love as much as possible. As he learns to crawl, he learns to love small pebbles, Gerber's beef stew, his brother's G.I. Joe, pieces of small change, bits of lint, and small sections of linoleum from the kitchen floor.

This is the most naive, unformed sort of love, and we spend the bulk of our lives refining it. We learn to love our Brownie Troops, our pets, our country, various bodacious foxes upon the television; and most perversely of all, ourselves.

Such is the paradox of love and attraction: Almost everyone from the moment of birth fears abandonment. And yet it is a true and tragic fact that many people who were "abandoned by a parent" in youth continue to repeat the pattern throughout their lives. Many men and women invariably choose partners who will hurt and neglect them because "they can't help themselves."

Women, when asked on questionnaires "What kind of man do you want in life?" invariably put check marks next to "Traveling salesman," "Pirate," and "Someone who used to be married to Princess Caroline of Monaco."

As a result, these women tend to become emotionally attached to the carbohydrate food group, which is a great source of solace in moments of despair. Carbohydrates never abandon anyone. They are always readily available at all-night gas stations on interstate highways. "Here we are," they say. "Driving all night to put a broken romance behind you? Have a Hostess Snoball for the road. Have a thousand."

Men have 50,000-watt call-in radio shows to serve this same essential function in their lives.

THE MODERN PROBLEM

You probably know, if you haven't been living under a rock the last ten years, that romance has gotten a whole lot more difficult as time has gone by. It used to be that everyone fell in love and got married as soon as it was legal, and there wasn't much you could write about it that would fill a half-page in an average drugstore novel.

Nowadays, everyone is what they used to call in France a "connoisseur."

Everyone is a Picky Little Devil, nowadays.

Dating in America usually goes through three distinct phases.

1) You meet someone who seems very, very special to you, and he or she says, "You know, I'm looking for someone really special in my life, and there is something . . . I don't know . . . *special* about you."
2) Two or three months go by, and your dream date says, "You know, you're a really nice person, but I'm just not looking for anyone 'special' right now."
3) You break up with your dream date and go your separate ways, and a month later you hear that your dream date has gotten married. He met someone . . . *special.*

This generally happens to you about eight or nine times in your life, before you get it right.

WHAT MAKES IT WORSE

After a broken romance, people have a tendency to say extraordinary things to you, such as that you can "learn" from bad experiences. (Who wants to even *know* the things that you "learn" from bad experiences?) And that the best thing to do after falling off a horse is to get right back on again. (The process of "getting right back on" extremely dangerous horses was a very effective means of population control, by the way, in Victorian England.)

All you can see when someone breaks up with you is that there are always obscene amounts of sunshine in the air, children are laughing and skipping, squirrels are doing euphoric *tours-jetés* through the grass, the marijuana pushers in the park are singing "Isn't It Romantic?" in the key of F-sharp, and every living being you see is looking deeply and longingly into the eyes of That Special Someone. You think mistily, "If only I could just take a flamethrower to this scene and incinerate everyone I see. . . ."

Men usually suffer a lot worse when breakups occur. They don't have the natural coping mechanisms women have—getting together in small groups late at night, dying their hair and eating too many onion rings. Men just mourn.

There are not too many original ways to mourn. If there were, everyone would like country music.

GETTING ROMANCE NAILED DOWN

When we finally do meet "that special someone," and the feeling appears to be *mutual,* the first thing we experience is a sense of childlike wonder, followed quickly by a sense of profound skepticism. Most of us don't really believe that any such awesomely fine human actually could or *should* be crazy about us; but eventually, if our beloved can manage to prove his or her eternal devotion to us, we do the next most logical thing.

We try to see how far we can push it.

Maybe this is a way of forestalling what we feel is the inevitable. . . . Did we get the idea from the movies, after all, or just real life, that nothing good ever lasts forever? Why does the wedding scene always come immediately before the scene of opening the letter with "the truth about Alexis"? Or with the car exploding at the bottom of the cliff?

Why is there something about a terribly happy photograph that seems to throw the willies into all of us?

If you are an avid reader of Star Bios, you know that the happiest possible photos are always the ones shrouded in black crepe, and captioned accordingly:

"Orson Welles and Rita Hayworth in Happier Times," they say.

"Lucille Ball and Cuban Bandleader Husband in Happier Times."

"George Sand and Frédéric Chopin in Happier Times."

"The crew of the *Lusitania* in Happier Times."

If you are looking at your own wedding pictures, and you can't help seeing "Lisa and Future Adulterer Husband Chuck in Happier Times," is there something wrong with you, or are you just a normal realistic member of the human race?

In most cases, the answer is usually "both."

But what the heck. Why do fools fall in love?

Probably because fools need to get married and have foolish children, who will produce foolish grandchildren; and this is what makes up the Grand Plan of Life.

And all the people of normal intelligence are more than content to be "close personal friends," and leave it at that.

Getting By with a Little Help

WE do not necessarily have to like the people we fall in love with (in fact, it makes better "daytime drama" if we don't), but we have to like our friends.

We are allowed to call and pester them during dinner once a month ("*Eating?* No, I'm just chewing. *Vous avez un problème,* Bud?") if they reserve the same privilege. They say romantic things to us, like "Let's get pregnant on the same day, Marilyn," and we get so excited by this prospect that we forget that getting pregnant all-too-often involves having and raising *actual children.* They say things like "I'm your friend and I love you, so I can ask you why your hair looks like a stuffed weasel."

Old friends do things like get married in Manitoba, and expect us to find a sitter, and then they get divorced the following week, and they say, "If you were my friend, you would have seen this coming."

Where did our "old friends" come from in the first place, and how did they rate this seniority?

It is safe to say that getting into trouble in Junior High School together is something that bonds two people for life. Especially since, when you were in Junior High School, teachers had a way of saying with an absolutely straight face words that sounded as if no one with a straight face ever ought to say them. (The "Diet of Worms"? "Pepin the *Short*"?) When you are thirteen, the name of just about everything and everyone sounds alternately strange and obscene to you ("Ethelred the Unready"? "Percy *Bysshe* Shelley"?) The next thing you knew, you were in shop class, discussing "male and female sockets" and "ball-peen hammers." ("Would the two of you in the back row mind standing up and telling the entire class what is so hysterically funny? Would the two of you mind *instructing* the class?")

The trouble is, by the time you're eighteen your hormones have simmered down to the point where your sense of humor is not nearly so all-inclusive. (It is a loss. You will never laugh so hard in your life again.)

Anyway, that's where friendship begins. It never gets better than this.

Nowadays, it's hard to have real friends. The reasons for this are not dissimilar from the ones people give for being constantly thwarted in romance:

"EVERYONE IS DIFFERENT THESE DAYS. EVERYONE IS JUST SO COMPETITIVE."

Probably one of the most fascinating advertising slogans of all time is the glad cry "Be the envy of all your friends!" Everything about this slogan implies that nuclear war would be a step up in the evolution of the human race.

Few people are capable of envying someone *and* liking him or her personally at the same time. If we needed to explain this slogan to foreigners (which one hopes will never happen), we could rightfully paraphrase it as: "Be the bane-of-existence of all your friends," or "Be the subject of vicious gossip among all your friends," or "Say *¡Adios, muchachos!* to all your friends."

It is hard to imagine what product or service one would be so venal as to covet to the point of eradicating all one's friendships. And yet, day by day, many Americans comb the countryside in search of exactly such products and services; and then wonder why no one ever calls them anymore.

FRIENDSTYLES

But some clever people try to circumvent crass competitiveness by inventing new styles of friendship that are consistent with an eighties, Hell-who's-got-the-time? kind of thinking.

FRIENDSHIP A LA CARTE

In order to envision "A la Carte Friends," you have to think of existence as a restaurant you can't really afford to eat at. So you tend to choose friends who are digestible and affordable, and most important, who look nice together lying on the plate.

In other words, it is not a bad idea to have a number of attractive, superficial friends to fill a number of different functions. Superficial people always have something to talk about because they don't waste a lot of time letting neurological impulses reach their cerebral cortex for interpretation. If you have friends who are Jesuit priests or Ming Dynasty scholars, they hardly ever want to talk to you about Mariel Hemingway's breast implants, or anything else of interest to many A la Carte people.

If you have a number of A la Carte Friends, it is a very good idea to have "call waiting" installed on your telephone line. This is a very subtle and successful way of saying to people, "I have someone just as superficial, but *much more entertainingly so,* on my other line, so you will have to go away now." And you know that a really good A la Carte Friend will perform this same favor for you, the next time you call him up to chat. Or her. Always ask what your A la Carte Friend is wearing when you talk to her on the telephone, so that she will not develop the uncomfortable impression that you *somehow care about her as a person.* Because then she would be obliged to call you back and care about your knee problem.

THE ITALIAN-OPERA-CURTAIN-CALL SCHOOL OF FRIENDSHIP

This is a popular FriendStyle which espouses the theory that our lives fall into a series of consecutive acts and scenes, and it is best to choose our friends accordingly. In most Italian operas, there are a number of characters who have a predictably short life expectancy, due to finding swords in their backs, being jailed by Nefarious Viscounts, and other misfortunes; so in order to give these folks a fair shake, they are allowed to take a bow at the end of their particular act, rather than at the end of the opera. In our lives, it is not unusual for us to allow our friends to take a bow and then head into the wings, especially when we have a new tenor we would like to audition.

After all, most of us are not living on the plains of Kansas anymore, and there are thousands of people out there who *could* be our friend. Maybe Mary Lou Retton or Keith Richards or Lee Iacocca would like to be our friend. Who knows? We could meet them in a movie line, and they might say, "You're a pretty interesting little s.o.b." And then we would have to say, "New act. Time to retire the old friends."

Besides, it's hard enough to have to remember our old friends' kids' birthdays; not to mention where they moved to after Pennzoil bought out their home office back in '83, or maybe it was '82. And of course, every time we see them, it's amazing how much older they've gotten than *we* have.

Since most of us are affluent enough to pay mourners to attend our funerals when the time comes, the need for "old, dear" friends has just about vanished from our lives.

The only thing sad about this is that there'll be no one waiting up for us in the Percy Bysshe Shelley suite in Heaven when the Afterlife calls us.

Family Life Today: Gateway to Serious Worrying

If you are one of those people who have decided not to have children, people always want to ask you, "Why not?" No one ever asks you, "Why don't you want to be Pope?" "Why don't you want to wave adieu to careless youth?" "Why don't you want to have your teeth filed down to razor-like points, and go over Niagara Falls in a teacup?"

All these activities, like the decision to have children, involve high risk, a loss of self-determination, and no small amount of megalomania.

And yet every year millions of folks take the plunge, and find themselves happily aswim in wallet-size photos they swore they would never torture their friends with. Their reasons for having children don't "make sense," nor are they supposed to. Volcanoes and classical symphonies and asthma attacks don't "make sense." They're just part of the eternal natural order of life.

The list of reasons people give for having children reads like a "Who's Who" of human foibles, and is a touching article of faith in and of itself.

We want to pass something "immortal" on to the world.

Sooner or later you will die. You have a mind that is unique; you play the clarinet like an angel; you have haunting eyes and fabulous hair and an overbite unlike any other; and the loss of all these things from the gene pool would be a tragedy.

Children fill you with the miracle of life.

You had another chance once, in your youth. When you visited the chicken hatchery on the third-grade field trip, you did not have an appropriately profound reaction to the yellow glop which is "the stuff of life itself," and you asked to be excused. So Fate is giving you a second chance.

We owe it to future generations.

For most of the sixties and seventies there were too many people living on the planet, and we saw a lot of scary aerial shots of the beaches of Rio de Janeiro, where things were so crowded hardly anyone could get a suntan anymore.

Now everybody is scared there won't be *enough* of us in the near future; or that there won't be enough of the right *kinds* of us, because in the last ten years, no one was having children, or it was being done by all the wrong people. If *we don't act now,* in the future everyone in the world (us) will be either in an old folks' home or in nursery school, and there will only be three or four people in their mid-twenties, and they will have to do *all* the shopping and legwork.

We need people on our side.

After about two years of even the happiest marriage, "just the two of you" gets a little claustrophobic. Your spouse begins to remind you that you haven't got the sense that God gave geese—and he or she begins to address him-or-herself to this fact at regular intervals. And when you say things like "So what makes *you* so smart, Charlene?" you realize that as a landmark argument summation, this is not exactly Oliver Wendell Holmes–caliber material, and you end up feeling sort of glum because your side isn't making any progress.

This is the exact moment we often decide to procreate. *We need recruits.* Moments after birth, we begin to lure our children over to our side with lucid arguments, which they are scarcely in any position to contradict. (This is why, at heart, we are *all* Mommy's or Daddy's—wearing Mommy's or Daddy's official insignia, helping shoot down Daddy's or Mommy's psychic B-1 bombers, and getting extra ice cream on the sly whenever we've done a good day's work.)

Of course, there's a lot of loose talk around these days about "consistent" parenting, which is meant to give a child a well-rounded, holistic sense of himself. "Problems" are said to occur when parents are either too strict or too lazy, too permissive or too rigid; one parent says black, the other says white. But this is why we were given dolls and pets to practice on as children. What is more instructive than to have a tea party with our kitten, smack him when he knocks over his saucer, kiss him on the ears and say we're sorry; then throw him across the room when he bites us in the face? These are the building blocks from which we learn.

THE BIGGEST PLUNGE

Much has been written about women being torn between motherhood and their careers; and most of it has been reprinted and Xeroxed and tacked up on somebody's bulletin board, so you have probably read it all. The same woman wrote all of it, anyway.

A lot of women who have never been pregnant before are understandably unsure about the suddenness of its impact. They are afraid they may have a sudden out-of-the-blue craving one day and suddenly shout to their secretary, "Cancel that board meeting at ten, Minnie! I'm going to sit home on my couch for thirty-six weeks and watch game shows!" (It is not quite this sudden, although if you *ever* catch yourself watching *The Price Is Right* on purpose, you are quite seriously pregnant, and possibly even in labor.)

A lot of women think that staying home (and having kids) means somehow being doomed to enjoy housework to the end of all eternity. And no wonder. Consider the plight of women on television commercials. They have a horrible jolly quality that has never waned since 1955. In ever-increasing numbers they are forced to perform Broadway Dance Routines while cleaning their toilet bowls.

And maybe you've thought of this: Scientists have determined that common "household dust" contains particles that have traveled to earth from BILLIONS and BILLIONS of miles away in space. Fragments of the rings of Saturn, bits of supernovae, comet scraps, the sands of Pluto, the powdered atoms of constellations; all the busywork of the universe lying on your windowsill, crying out to be sifted and catalogued. And what did your grandmother do, but whip out a big old dust rag and THROW IT ALL IN THE TRASH CAN. For thousands of years women have been destroying valuable evidence about the origins of the universe that Carl Sagan would ransom his turtleneck to get his hands on.

If you wonder why women are even taking the time to be confused by issues like this, it has to do with an affliction known among scientists as "Role Hysteria"—the sudden, nagging question that torments women every decade or so and runs, "What is my *role* in life now, and how am I almost certainly managing to screw it up?"

Eskimo women, when they have outlived their usefulness, know that the proper recourse is to wander out onto an ice floe to perish. And many modern women carry around an image of their husbands arriving at a dinner party with a covered dish, saying, "Betty couldn't make it tonight; she's gone out on an ice floe to perish. But here's the casserole she prepared as her last living act."

PONDERING THE IRREVOCABLE

You have probably taken at least five minutes out of your workday to reflect on the responsibility of putting another human being through the process known as: BIRTH.

"Birth Trauma" is not just a fancy name that someone made up. There one is in an unborn state, taking a relaxing snooze in the well-known FETAL POSITION, and suddenly, quite without warning, all the forces of nature conspire to expel one out into the cold. The obstetrician is standing out there like the guy with the bullhorn in the old Jimmy Cagney movies, saying, "WE KNOW YOU'RE IN THERE! COME OUT NICELY WITH YOUR HANDS UP!" And this is your first instance of knowing that life is far from a low-pressure issue. The first human being you will see will be the obstetrician in a green paper muu-muu, attaching oversized barbecue tongs to your skull. And then he slaps you around a little, and then someone fills out a form where it specifies "M" or "F." And this "M" or "F" business is something you'll have to grapple with for the entire length of your existence.

A THRILLING BEGINNING

As a parent, the minute you bring a new life into the world, you realize you've never really understood the meaning of ANXIETY before. Worrying about *yourself* was just an *hors d'oeuvre.* Now you've made it to the *main course,* people.

Eating and bathing, for example, used to be sort of a rote activity. Now you are troubled by claims that "Ivory Soap is 99.44% Pure." Pure *what,* for God's sake? Pure toxicity? Pure Liquid Death?

You become convinced the entire world is trying to tell you that you are a terrible parent. There's Annette Funicello on TV telling you "*Choosy* mothers choose Jif." And you find yourself attacking the TV screen, yelling, "I'm *sure* I'm going to take nutritional advice from someone who spent almost all her formative years wearing *mouse ears. . . .*"

Many parents think, "What if my baby falls off the changing table when I'm not watching, and it grows up to be able to pronounce only words beginning with 'D,' and spends its entire life watching *Laverne and Shirley* in syndication?"

Lighten up, okay?

Just imagine the mental list you have which contains all the things you *swore you would never do when you had children.*

You will do all those things, okay? Everybody does all those things.

Now you can get on with your life.

YOU SWORE YOU WOULD NEVER BE AN OVERPROTECTIVE, GERM-CRAZED KILLJOY

You can probably still remember the age when you yourself used to enjoy playing "Riverboat Captain," by launching small objects into the storm drain, building keen dams out of mud, and floating Popsicle sticks into the sewer, to test current ebb and flow and other exciting aspects of natural science.

And your mother always came running out the door, saying, "Get out of that filth! You don't know where it's *been*!" (And you know perfectly well where it's *been.* It's been in the gutter. Where else does most quality filth come from?) And yet you too will say these exact words when the time comes.

YOU SWORE YOU WOULD NEVER CHANNEL YOUR THWARTED AMBITIONS THROUGH A HELPLESS INFANT

Everyone wants "what's best" for their children.

But in the last thirty years, ominous rumblings have been heard about increasing a child's "cognitive development," or "smarts," at a very early age. In fact, one of the great advantages to being in the womb these days is that no one has figured out a way to show an unborn child "flash cards" to increase his pre-reading skills. Give them time on this one.

There's a war on now between the followers of Dr. Spock, who believe that horsing around with a puppy once a week or so will get a kid's synapses hippy-hopping well enough to boot him into junior high, and those who believe it is every parent's job to bring out the *true genius* in every baby. (Get those mobiles over that crib! *Play that kid some Bruckner!*)

As a parent, you don't really have to buy into all this stuff, and you *can* say, "Heck, I'm going to bring up my kid *normal.* Speaking *one* Indo-European language at age six is good enough for me!" But how do you buttress yourself against your friend who's chain-smoking again because she's been up all week helping her kid cram for his nursery-school entrance exam? Because if he doesn't get into that nursery school, he won't get into Andover, and then the admissions committee at Stanford will laugh in his face, and he'll die in the gutter, a broken, wasted husk at age nineteen. (You laugh. How many words did *your* kid speak at eleven months? Were they *polysyllabic* words? Ask your kid to spell "polysyllabic." He *can't*?)

YOU SWORE YOU WOULD NEVER BE AN OVERPROTECTIVE KILLJOY, PART II

It is hard to be cool when your PRECIOUS BABY'S whole life is at stake every minute of the day that he is out of your sight.

When you used to come home very late from football practice, or whatever, your mother, if she was like most mothers, would say something like "Oh, thank God. I was just beginning to worry."

Beginning to worry implies several ominous things. In the old days, mothers didn't have aerobics and night-school classes to go to, so they worked on worrying as a career. This career would assume phases, such as:

- PHASE I: Beginning to Worry.
- PHASE II: *Succeeding* at Worrying.
- PHASE III: Calling several friends and neighbors for a session of Group Worrying.

Even after famous admiral John Paul Jones came home late from battling the British (and saying, "I Have Just Begun to Fight"), his mother met him at the hitching post, saying, "Zounds, John Paul—I had just begun to worry."

Mothers are almost always afraid that their children see things or do things or hear things that will traumatize them and "give them nightmares," but in reality it is probably mothers themselves that have the nightmare industry sewn up.

For what it's worth, most of the horror films turned out these days feature special effects so sophisticated and realistic that anything kids see in an actual nightmare pales by comparison. Most children lie there thinking, "Come *on.* No monster from the Pits of Hell has teeth like *that.* Those teeth are totally wrong." And if he could ask for a Dream Refund upon awakening, he probably would.

Feel better? Just a *little*?

Success! What's Stopping *You?*

It's a well-known saying: "Those who can, do. Those who can't, become Amway distributors."

There's no trick to becoming a very great success in America. But there is a "secret." If you have a "secret," then you can be a success. It doesn't really matter what the secret is; all you have to do is take out an ad in the back pages of your favorite family, beauty, or gun magazine, with a picture of yourself, saying "KNOWN SUCCESS REVEALS SECRET," and watch the letters pour in.

Some people have actually done a little legwork and found out, say, the secret to making Crisco taste like butter (or at least the secret to making celebrities go on TV and *say* that Crisco tastes like butter), but that step isn't really necessary.

The best way to be a real success is to be it "overnight," "in your spare time," and "at a cost of only pennies a day."

Another thing that you can try is working.

What you need to know of course, is *which fields* of endeavor are showing the most promise over the long haul. Master them; and then nothing and no one can stop you, no matter how hard they try:

BED 'N' BREAKFAST TYCOON

A recent, upbeat trend in America is that many of America's scenic, historic homes are being bought up by young couples with the time, energy, and relentless imagination to restore them. The majority of these scenic homes are being turned into scenic "real estate offices," so that they can be used to sell even more scenic, historic homes; and projections indicate that by the year 1993, there will be more scenic, historic real estate offices than there are homes in America. (In fact, it is estimated that by the year 2009, the entire state of Massachusetts will have its real estate license; at which point it could lawfully attempt to sell the state of Rhode Island to the state of Connecticut, as a condominium, with an attractive financing deal. The tenants would have the ATLANTIC OCEAN to swim in, although a larger pool would eventually be constructed.)

The bed 'n' breakfast movement has landed on us like a 900-pound Laura Ashley comforter, and it strikes us as a stunning yet welcome reversal in the hospitality industry.

Years ago they were called "tourist homes" and run by aged ladies with purple hair, only nobody wanted to stay there when they could check into spanking-new (and convenient) motels. Only later, nobody wanted to stay in motels anymore because they were spanking-new (and faceless) and had the same prints of fruit markets in Tijuana on all the walls. And besides, nobody knew how many traveling salesmen had slept in the beds in the company of cocktail waitresses with beehive hairdos.

And then an idea came over from England, known as the "bed 'n' breakfast." Only the original tourist-home "Mom" and "Pop" are now living in retirement communities in Boca Raton; and 86 percent of the quaint bed 'n' breakfasts in the state of New Hampshire are now run by a nice young couple named Chip and Estelle Beecham-Horowitz who used to live downstairs in your building.

The best thing about buying and visiting property in the country is that you can spend weekends driving through covered bridges, observing "colorful locals," and "leafing."

Best of all, you can attend "tag sales." (You can roughly translate the phrase "Let's go to a tag sale, honey" as "Let's go buy some dishes and furniture that poor people are ashamed to have in their houses." It's an interesting exercise in applied anthropology.)

Of course, owning country property means being subject to the vicissitudes of nature: storms, plagues of locusts, too much frost and no heat, too much rain but no snow. But going *out of business* at a charming country establishment is a great American tradition. In the movie *White Christmas,* Bing Crosby goes to entertain at an inn owned by his old C.O. from the Army, only to find that there will be no snow for Christmas and no one has checked in. And before Bing even gets to sing "White Christmas" (which you may even have guessed he was going to sing in this movie. *Did you guess?*), he sings a song called "What Can You Do with a General when He Stops Being a General?"—a song that had America dancing and clapping its hands for many months after the movie came out.

Even if you are not lucky enough to own a bed 'n' breakfast, people have a way of thinking you've "really made it" when you go to live in the country; and all the people you used to know in the city drive out in Hertz cars to visit you with their kids and, better yet, their laundry.

"SERVICE" INDUSTRIALIST

According to modern adherents of Darwin, when all other life forms have died off in the future, the only creatures that will remain will be worker ants, roaches, segmented worms, and the people holding the service contracts on your cars and home appliances.

It is estimated that ten years from now, a 1997 Toyota Corolla liftback will retail for about seven times what it does now. The service contract (otherwise known as "Fear Insurance") on said vehicle will cost you $750,000.

The more devices we operate, the more "technicians" we need to keep those devices in order; the more goods we purchase, the more "sales technicians" we need to aid us in the purchase of said goods.

For example, if we decide to spend the day at Macy's "trying on sweaters," we cannot expect to accomplish this task without the aid of skilled "dressing-room technicians" —those unsung individuals who stand outside dressing-room doors and hand out indispensable "plastic numbers" to remind us of HOW MANY GARMENTS we're considering at any given moment. *You could be one of them* if you master the necessary skills. Professional "Plastic-Number Guardians" must be ever-vigilant, dealing as they do with pinpoint accuracy and state-of-the-art GARMENT-TRYING PRECISION. They spend hours perfecting the assiduous chewing of sugarless gum, and ingeniously combine this motor skill with the GLAZED STARE OF A DEAD TROUT; and they must do all this on *one* pair of support hose a day.

Classes in this rewarding field are filling fast; are *you* the kind of gal who has what it takes?

Check your local Yellow Pages.

DESIGNER-CHICKEN EXECUTIVE

Nothing was ever quite the same after Frank Perdue broke the news on the American airwaves in the late seventies that "It Takes a Tough Man to Make a Tender Chicken."

And no wonder. A chicken makes a strong partisan statement, without raising anyone's life-insurance rates or ravaging their arteries. Chicken is one of the few foods a man can sell to Americans anymore and still look himself in the eye while shaving in the morning.

So what if poultry executives have to spend a lot of time with herky-jerky little barnyard fowl who are no less intelligent when their heads happen not to be attached to them? (This particular characteristic makes chickens in no way inferior to many humans.)

There is an inevitable grandeur that rubs off on you when you associate with chickens and rise from Chicken Executive to full-blown POULTRY CELEB.

Soon, you can have the pleasure of lurking around supermarkets and overhearing career women saying, "Is this a *Leon Katz* chicken?" And you can almost certainly become a national symbol of virility and entrepreneurship by doing your own TV commercials. You can choose the models who will bite into your succulent thigh-meat on-camera and say, "I looked a long time for a LEON."

You will be on a perch of your own—one of the few—the proud—the CHICKEN-HEARTED.

NAMER OF SOAP-OPERA CHARACTERS

The scarcity of new, provocative names for daytime-soap-opera characters is a problem reaching epidemic proportions.

Nothing ever happens to people on soap operas named "Ann," "Dick," and "Sue."

It was long ago made a prerequisite in Soap Opera Law that all *significant* soap-opera characters should be named after, if at all possible:

- States
- State capitals
- Fragrances
- Roman senators, or, at the very least,
- Eras in geologic history

Without names like "Argentina," "Palomino," "Brick," "Cicero," "Lolita," and "Eudoxia," soap-opera characters can hardly be expected to have the energy to do all the flouncing, prancing, husband-stealing, and falling-off-pretend-precipices that is expected of them on a day-to-day basis.

BUT ALL THE POSSIBLE NAMES ARE BEING TAKEN VERY, VERY QUICKLY. (Two major, respectable networks were caught fighting over "Tigris-Euphrates" recently. Until they discovered that also negotiating for it were Nabisco, CBS, and Ford Motor Co. It will probably be late next year before we discover whether "Tigris-Euphrates" will be Becky and Preston's illegitimate son, or a luxury sedan.)

Being a namer of soap-opera characters is a high-paying

field, but not one you can pursue in your spare time, since the hours are long and the work is bruising. The minimum professional background required is two years' screenwriting or directing experience; a year of geokinetic physics; and five years' experience naming *either* feminine-protection products or floor polishes.

JUDITH KRANTZ HEROINE

Perhaps Judith Krantz, more than any other social historian, has given the modern woman something to strive for.

There are women out there whose size-4 Charles Jourdan shoes *you* could fill, Little Miss, if only you would dry off and climb out of that typing pool and INTO THE LIFE YOU WERE REALLY MEANT FOR.

First of all, there are a lot of people out there who are dukes and barons and marchionesses and *know* it and behave accordingly; but there are certain OTHER people out there whose fathers just happen to have been the King of Montenegro, only they've just sort of forgotten about it for now, and so they are working at K-Mart sticking the price tags on plastic swimming pools because they can never forgive their half-brother, Boris, for revealing that terrible secret about their past in the pages of *Vanity Fair.* WHO'S TO SAY THIS COULDN'T BE *YOU*?

There's nothing wrong with having a title or family fortune, and throwing it in the toilet for a few years, and deciding to reclaim it years and years later when you bloody well feel like it.

There's nothing wrong with having unconscionable amounts of money. (Unlike the "Instant Winners" you see doing TV commercials for Publishers Clearing House, you will not have to spend your entire adult life under sedation, or, worse, pretending to be a close personal friend of Ed McMahon.)

The Best and Worst of Leisure

NONE of the Founding Fathers could have guessed at what America has become today: a nation driven mad by the scent of leisure. A nation that works hard, plays harder, when necessary PLAYS TO KILL.

The Founding Fathers would have said, "Idle hands are the devil's badminton racquet," and they would have been right. Year after year, more and more Americans are turned loose on the highways, fairways, lakes, and restaurants of America (not to mention the highways, fairways, lakes, and restaurants of the world). Give them a fishing license, a lift ticket, a passport, a menu, and a map of Montana; and get out of their way.

FRANCIS X. BUSHMAN'S REAL MIDDLE NAME . . . AND WORSE

You can argue that a civilized society identifies itself by the board games it plays. (The twenties grit and greed of *Monopoly*; the bracing Cold War paranoia of *Risk* and *Stratego* . . .)

Nowadays, the parlor games that count are the ones that feed and fixate on TRIVIA. In other words, we are living in an AGE OF INFORMATION, BUT THAT INFORMATION NEED NOT NECESSARILY PERTAIN TO *OTHER INFORMATION*. In other words, you may or may not be required to show photos of your three adorable children at the next dinner party you attend, but you will be expected to know which are the three landlocked countries of South America.* Knowing which three countries of South America are landlocked could only be considered *not trivial* if you happened to be a wholesaler of trawlers or beach towels.

There have been accusations that Trivial Pursuit is a white, elitist sport (and indeed, many individuals in West Africa are forced to wait weeks and weeks for available copies of Trivial Pursuit, and many have to buy it on the Black Market in return for packages of Gauloises, or kegs of sorghum flour).

But even white elitist dilettantes put a lot of sweat and mental elbow grease into memorizing Gertrude Ederle's best swimming time across the English Channel and the number of dots on a standard set of dominoes.

HYBRID EATING

Now that people have more leisure time than ever before, they are beginning to invent new, *amusant* ways to fill that time (and very particularly, their mouths) by finding brand-new excuses to EAT VERY MUCH FOOD, and to give these "excuses" a name—as in "brunch," which is what Famous Botanist Luther Burbank would have gotten by crossing breakfast with lunch (thank God no one did it the other way and crossed lunch with breakfast, which would give you "lruckfast," and does not sound at all like the kind of meal you would like to drink mimosas during.)

Those people who do not enjoy going out to restaurants are, of course, quite justified in staying home, provided it does not trouble them to know that the *entire world* is out there moving, shaking, sparkling, and passing them by.

One reason "off-hour" eating has gained so much popularity lately is that it is increasingly difficult to simply call up

* (Look it up yourself.)

a restaurant and tell them when you would like to come and visit them. First they laugh very politely, or else snort ever-so-delicately into the phone, and then they proceed to tell you when they are prepared to *let* you come. "Thursday night," they say, "we have a seating at five P.M. and one at one A.M." Do not for a minute think that they are bluffing you on this one.

One reason people are very wary of "status" restaurants is that they occasion the loss of one's self-determination, and specifically, one's car keys. Unless we live in Los Angeles and are used to valet parking, who among us wants to give our car keys to a total stranger who has a patch that says "FLASH" upon his pocket? In Los Angeles, no one is even hired as a parking valet unless he has an agent and a call-back for a *Movie of the Week* audition the next day. This is far less likely to be the case in Indianapolis or most chowder houses east of the Rockies.

Most restaurants nowadays have shortened their menus to less than a page in length, but this is for a very specific reason. With competition for restaurant patronage at a premium, waiters and waitresses are compelled to give an Abbreviated Customer Intelligence Test, otherwise known as the "List of Specials," and woe betide anyone who cannot pass this crucial interrogation the first time.

No one knows where the results of this testing are duly sent, but it is roughly similar to breaking the bank at Monte Carlo; every time an eatery has a customer who *actually remembers* the "List of Specials," the list is automatically lengthened. There is a restaurant in Dobbs Ferry, New York, that once had a list of 798 specials. Several elderly patrons had to be carried out while the "List of Specials" was being recited, due to heat exhaustion and mental fatigue. The sauces alone took 35 minutes.

It is no wonder that most patrons are completely cowed by the menu offerings of most popular restaurants. ("Cowed," in particular, by the serious amounts of *goat* cheese showing up in things like hors d'oeuvres, salads, and, yes, pizza. Let's get one thing straight here: Say *fromage de chèvre* till you foam at the chops, but we are talking about cheese made from an animal that eats used flashlight batteries for breakfast.)

STUPID WATER SPORTS

Americans will pay through the nose to be near water; they thrill to propel themselves into it and through it; but nothing can quite beat the wind-in-the-nostrils euphoria of *standing on top of it.*

Waterskiing is fraught with a number of real physical perils, but none of them is greater than the possibility that at the moment of truth, when we sail like a swan over the surface of the water, let go of the tow rope with one hand, and wave gaily, NO ONE WILL BE WATCHING ADMIRINGLY.

Henry David Thoreau himself posed the question "Indeed, if I am waterskiing on Walden Pond, and no one is present to watch me gaily wave, then do I exist?"

Decapitation is also a fairly constant problem. Whoever is driving the motorboat is usually on his fourteenth Michelob, and when he makes a bank turn (forgetting that this is summer and he is not driving a snowmobile) he will manage to neatly lop off your head while you are waving frantically from the water.

This is why the performers at Cypress Gardens are always wearing those decorative headpieces. So they'll be visible from the water. Year after year in our lakes and rivers, *tiaras save lives.*

MUSH, BIFFY

Nowadays, people wonder what kinds of activities are left for a family to enjoy together. People in the movies are doing things with firearms, and their tongues, that most minors (and probably most adults) should be left unaware of.

Winter sports like skiing have gained a lot of popularity of late: the simple art of enjoying the wilderness while wearing boards on your feet and a great deal of underwear. The main point of skiing is to locomote yourself as fast as you can, so that you create a layer of "perspiration" between your skin and your underwear, and when you stop in the woods for a refreshing snack, the layer of moisture freezes to your body, and Dad makes light of the fact by telling amusing "hypothermia" stories. Cross-country skiing was invented by the Norwegians to commemorate (and simulate) the deaths of the British Antarctic Expedition of 1912. Indeed, while skiing only 5 kilometers from a 7-Eleven, small children have been known to become delirious and say, "Let's eat the sled dogs, Mom."

THE THRALL OF THE WILD

Americans love to go on camping trips because they always have, and if you ask them *why* they love to go on camping trips, they will probably say, "Well, it's because we always have."

There is a smallish percentage of adults who believe in camping for all ages (they usually bear an uncommon resemblance to golden retrievers, and though they do not exactly have tails, they do always appear to be wagging themselves in some mysterious way). Then there is a large percentage of adults who believe devoutly in compulsory camping for all minor school-age children. Camping brings children closer to "the purity" that existed everywhere in America before the white man came and brought his smoke detectors and pants suits and Vuarnet sunglasses. It is important for children to *see* nature—to absorb "Indian lore" —to learn Indian songs and how to build campfires; to listen for the snap of twigs, take decorative scalps, and make pinecone java.

Most adults have wisely repressed their summer-camp experiences in order not to poison their children against what could be a wholesome, fun-filled, friend-filled "adventure of a lifetime." But these are some of the dangers that plague all children during their first summer-camp experiences:

Camp Is Many Children's First Experience Away from Home, in the Bush, out of Doors.

Summer camping for very young children is not dangerous *per se,* unless for some reason you happen to be *afraid* of *9-foot breathing zombies that live at the bottom of lakes and emerge each evening at twilight covered with slugs and maggots to feast on human flesh.*

Some of these monsters have hooks for arms; some of them are the spirits of dead campers, or the parents of dead campers. When you are eleven years old, no one needs to tell you that most dead things can walk, and see where they are going, even with algae and dead fish in their eyes. It is thought that they are lured by the siren scent of melted marshmallows and graham crackers.

Camping "Changes" a Person.

Camping is a curious phenomenon, in that it reduces "socialized" young people back to a fairly primitive state in only a matter of weeks. (It is thought that author William Golding got his idea for the pig-slaughter scene in *Lord of the Flies* from a summer he spent at a sleep-away overweight camp in the Berkshires.)

Children become conversant with Naked Fear when they learn to camp. (Or, more properly, Fear in a Wolverines Swim Team bathing cap and nose plugs.) And of course the threat of carnivorous *bears* is with us, no matter where we go or what we do. Even children who camp out in suburban areas run the risk of the more civilization-disposed species: Eastern brown bear, spotted Rhode Island bear, Ursus Safeway, and others of their genus. There are also the threats of drowning, gang sodomy, RAW-WEENIE TRICHINOSIS, BLISTERING SUNBURN, and intestinal parasites that now infest every sparkling babbling brook in America.

But it is generally agreed that the most terrifying thing that can ever happen at camp is to be stuck in the bus with the kids who want to sing EVERY SINGLE VERSE of "Ninety-Nine Bottles of Beer on the Wall." These children never get laryngitis. They never come up for air or get bored.

These children invariably grow up to do TV ads for car-leasing companies, which appear approximately every thirteen seconds during *Laura* or *Sands of Iwo Jima* on the Late Show.

You can recognize the sane children on any camp bus, because they are the ones who throw themselves under the wheels of the bus at about Verse Seventy-six.

Nowadays, children have become so twisted by Creature Comforts that it is difficult to imagine them having a "True Wilderness Experience" anymore. Many nine-year-olds refuse to go on nature hikes through the Chesapeake marshlands unless their parents hire them Sherpas.

Conveniently, the amount of nature left around begging to be enjoyed is dwindling so rapidly that the problem will probably, naturally, take care of itself.

BAD PHOTOGRAPHY: HOBBY OF THE FAITHFUL

The argument is made each year: Why restrict the sale of Japanese, American-made, or Kodak cameras? After all, cameras don't shoot bad photos—people do.

Each year, hotbeds of bad photography spring up around the country. In the national parks alone, it seems to be an epidemic.

- Last year, more than five million bad photographs of Old Faithful were taken, many in which the famous geyser was almost totally obscured by cowboy hats on the heads of mothers from Wheeling, West Virginia.
- Eight million bad photos were taken of the Statue of Liberty. (At least half of them are so bad, they can't always be distinguished from bad photographs of the Taj Mahal, which, after starvation and Sikh terrorism, is the third-biggest national problem in India.)
- Seven hundred brand-new cameras were accidentally dropped into Niagara Falls, with more than a thousand bad photographs of the *Maid of the Mist* still intact inside them.

No one has ever found an antidote for the dreaded phrase "You must come over and see the slides of our trip." Pretending to be dead has had only marginal results.

In order to understand the advent and popularization of bad photography in America, we need to trace the evolution of American travel itself—specifically THE AUTOMOBILE, without which all the scenic wonders of America would go forever untrampled.

ROAD TRIP! ROAD TRIP!

There is a time when the fate and earthly prospects of human children mix almost inextricably with those of German shepherds and golden retrievers—the moment of Going for a Ride with Mom and Dad in the Car.

A great many tongues hang out at such moments, followed by the starting of the engine, the raising of the garage door, the negotiating of the driveway, and then the relentless, sinking miasma of Not Being There Yet. (Yes, this particular phase of the journey has traditionally lasted the longest.)

Road travel has changed dramatically in the last few years. Unfortunately, though it is proving true that you can raise a child's I.Q. by buying him educational pull toys and reading him Joseph Conrad in the tub, you can actually *lower* his I.Q. by taking him for a long ride on America's Interstate Highways.

High-level sensory deprivation has long been recognized by human-rights activists as one of the most effective forms of torture and forced ultimate brain docility.

This is why we can be thankful for the vast number of SCENIC LOOKOUTS available at the side of America's roadways. And we have the various state Departments of Highways to thank for *labeling* these scenic lookouts for us, lest we miss them entirely, or mistakenly pull over to gaze at a vista which is completely lacking in suitable scenicity.

Pranksters once planted a "Scenic Lookout" sign in front of a Toxic Slag Retail Outlet on the New York State Thruway, and several families pulled over to have picnics and take photographs, before they were asked by the State Police to move on.

STAYING AMUSED DURING TRAVEL has traditionally been one of man's greatest challenges in the twentieth century. It is not enough to hear your father bang the steering wheel because you have just gotten stuck behind a Studebaker with two old ladies from Pennsylvania, and scream, *"They must be in comas. I don't understand why they are letting people in comas drive cars these days."* Hence, the welcome invention of Car Games, to feed the intellect and sedate the soul. When you and a sibling reach the age where you can puzzle out the 26 characters of the Roman alphabet on road signs, your mother will duly teach you the Alphabet Game, to get you out of her hair. If you are the oldest, you will automatically get the right-hand side of the car, and your sister will automatically lose, because from the left-hand side of the car, she can only see the *backs* of signs. (She will be about fourteen years old before she figures this out.)

When this game works out less than effectively, your mother will try the Keep-Your-Hands-to-Yourself-or-Die Game, which generally goes something like: If You Don't Stop Fighting, Daddy Will Have to Turn Around and Swat You All, and Then the Car Will Go off the Road and into a Ditch, and All of Us Will Be Killed.

Adults need ways to amuse themselves during travel too. One popular form of amusement is to ride in the passenger seat of a car, wince at every turn the driver makes, give free passing and braking advice, and say things like "You should have turned at the Chevron station; *you'll never find it now*" whenever possible.

This is a practice not nearly as *popular* as it is common. Why is it no one ever refuses a martini at a party saying, "No drinks tonight. *I'm backseat driving*"? This could be a case where *Sedation Saves Lives.*

THE AMERICAN ULTRASPORTSMAN

There is a small, but growing, segment of the population which somehow believes—despite war, crime, accidents, and pestilence—that LIFE IS STILL NOT DANGEROUS ENOUGH.

These are people who call themselves "NEW-STYLE AD-

VENTURERS." People who like to live, as they say, "close to the edge"—people who subscribe to *Outside* magazine; *Soldier of Fortune*; *Road and Track*; yes, and *Yachting*.

These people never shrink from danger, but rather *embrace* it; they press danger up against the wall and pump it manfully (and there are women doing this, which is hard for a lot of us to take).

- Every Memorial Day weekend in Indianapolis, thousands of licensed drivers gun their engines and *refuse to obey the speed limit;* and they are given *cash awards* for these public infractions.
- Every year, thousands of Americans burn up their muscle tissue, their fat reserve, their cardiac valves, and their gray matter in that grueling, multidisciplinary event known as the "Triathlon."
- Every year a father from Cincinnati tells the world he is going to climb the world's six highest mountain peaks, and when they tell him, "It's been done," he says, "Fine. I'm going to climb the world's six highest *underwater* mountain peaks." Without oxygen.

Everyone "admires" people who are this publicly stupid. The closer they come to almost Crashing in Flames, the more people say, "*How I Wish I Could Be He!* Where is my hot-air balloon? There is still time left this season to cross the South Pole on roller skates."

No one knows what makes these people different from the rest of us. If there are ever *conclusive* studies done on this subject, let us all hope that the results are repressed.

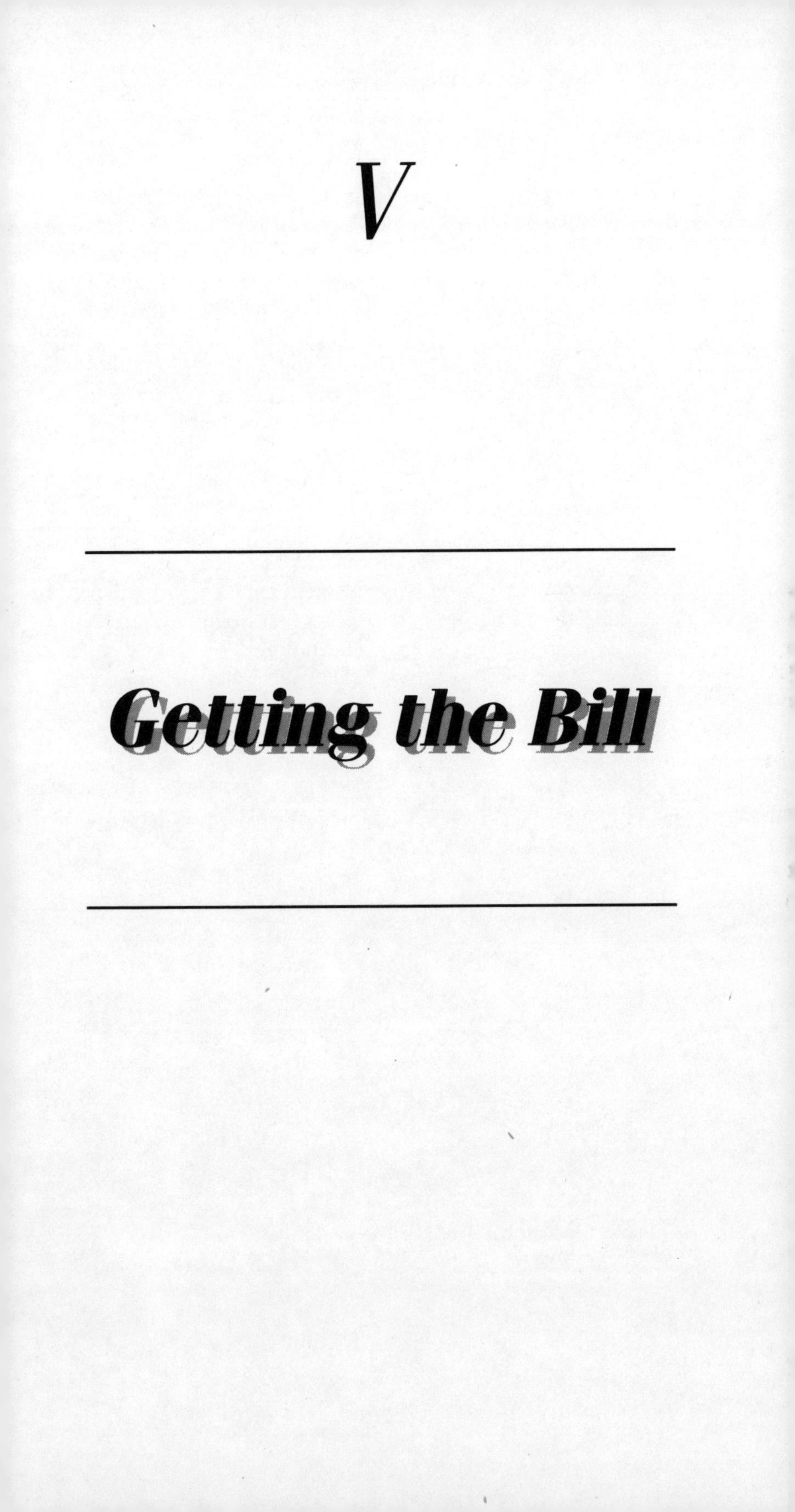

V

Getting the Bill

Senior Citizenship: You Too Can Someday Qualify

No wonder we fear getting old. We live in a dangerously youth-obsessed society. There are people who honestly care how Ricky Schroeder feels about continued U.S. aid to Nicaraguan rebels.

The main function that old people seem to serve nowadays is to appear on television advertisements for "old-fashioned," "down-home classic," and "country-style" foods. Nobody *really* cares what anybody said or did or *thought* in the "olden days," but we seem to have become extremely jealous and possessive about what people *ate*. If you close your eyes just for a split second, you can sort of imagine your grandmother made those Pepperidge Farm "Down Home Style Donuts," even though your grandmother is presently a cocktail waitress in Atlantic City.

Old people seem to make us a little bit nervous, because we're so conscious of them edging ever closer to mortality, and we know that there are really only two tried-and-true methods of Edging Ever Closer to Mortality. Living a Stupid Life is one (not wearing seat belts, hang gliding, and eating Japanese puffer fish, for example). Living a Long Life is the other.

Some people think of longevity as simply an act of PASSIVE AGGRESSION. It's possible, but unlikely, that you've had constant boatloads of fun, so that you *could* liken it, in a way, to the feeling one has after winning a baseball game only because the other team never bothered to show up.

Obviously, this isn't the charitable view of things by a long shot.

THE BEGINNINGS OF OLDNESS

On a man's thirty-ninth birthday, he usually asks that only the next-of-kin be notified.

He eyes his teenage nephew wistfully and says, "Casey, you're young, you've still got your arm, you're an impetuous moron; you're all the things I can never be again," and the two men go out for some brewskis, and rip some bar napkins to shreds and throw them at the TV screen.

Probably the high point of any "mature" person's life is the moment when a young person comes up and says to you, "You know, you've always been my *hero,* Uncle Jerry." (This is becoming less and less likely to happen all the time. Nowadays, it's much more likely they'll come up and say, "I think of you as my *mentor*"; or worse, "I would like you to be my *role model.*" And you feel terribly fearful that this honor is going to somehow involve written homework assignments.)

On a man's seventieth birthday, he decides he was just kidding about being old on his other birthdays, because he wasn't really *that* old. If a man's wife is still kicking around, he pinches her behind for emphasis; and if he gets to be eighty, he pinches *anybody's* behind for emphasis.

By the Agreed-On Rules, every eighty-year-old man is allowed to do all the things that civilization has spent the last millennium evolving past.

A MISCONCEPTION

A lot of problems began with the seemingly harmless expression "You're only as old as you feel."

It was generally intended that people would follow the *honor system* in buying into this expression and that the population would spread itself out *evenly* as to "feeling" the general spectrum of ages. As in:

"I feel about fifty-five, thanks."

"Gosh, I'm bouncing along at fifteen-and-a-half."

"I feel exactly sixty-five; not a day younger, not a day more."

But, of course, this isn't what happened at all.

A lot of people got greedy and insisted on feeling "eighteen," and refused to share "eighteen" with anybody else, and NOBODY ever said, "Well, I feel about eighty-nine, and is this really GREAT, or what?" Almost the entire population has settled into "feeling" early-to-mid twenties, and the lone voices in the crowd who honestly believe "life begins at fifty" are difficult to hear at all.

Maybe it's because we're in such awfully "good shape," but we prefer to think that age is the sort of commodity we can exercise an option on. As if they drove birthdays around in a little ice cream truck, door-to-door, and we could say, "No, thanks. Not this year." And we feel sort of hoodwinked when they descend upon us anyway. "Next year," we say, "we're going to stop answering that damned *bell.*"

CATCHING THE DOWNWARD CURVE

There is probably a just and humanitiarian reason for the fact that our senses start to deteriorate, like the old drive trains on automobiles, when we start to age. Your eyesight makes everything look like *Elvira Madigan,* and you say *What?* a lot. You are not necessarily the last to know you're getting older, but you're definitely the last to *hear* about it. ("I'm *what*? I'm getting *molder*?")

And then you start to worry about your other faculties. You fear you may be losing your grip. (Which is to say your *golf* grip, but at the same time, intimations of enfeeblitude don't have a terribly jolly effect on your morning. You just saw on the TV where there is some new essential vitamin or mineral that you should have been getting since the age of twenty-eight, and the idea of getting into a time machine and re-eating about 7,826 meals just seems like too tiring a thing to bother with anymore.) And every time you sneeze violently, your internal organs seem to say, "Let's have that one be the last of *those,* okay?"

On the bright side of getting older, people tend to make a big fuss about you doing all the little things that anyone else does in a normal day: "He reads the newspaper and *ties his shoes,*" everyone tells each other in triumph. People only make a fuss about literacy and shoe-tying at six and eighty-six. You wonder why they never do it in-between.

Actually, "eighty-six" is a much preferable age to "six" in one crucial area: you can throw a dinner roll at your unredeemed slug of a daughter-in-law, and everyone will say, "Now, *there's* a person who knows his mind." Try this sort of thing at age six, and they immediately say, "Now, *there's* a person who wants a thorough spanking."

ANOTHER GOOD THING

Another good thing is the welcome discovery that you have outlived most of the people who used to pester the bejeezus out of you. When you get old, you start talking to yourself, because of course you realize that there isn't anyone else around who says anything worth listening to. When you get even older, you start to *answer.* (At first, it isn't anything serious. You just say, "I'm going to go upstairs now and get that nice blue cardigan from Higbee's." Even though there isn't anyone around to say, "*That's* the ticket, Mary Elizabeth. *Go* for it.") You talk to chipmunks in the yard, you apologize to furniture for bumping into it. That kind of thing.

Later on, it gets more sophisticated. You start telling Tina on *One Life to Live* to wear a bra more often.

At least once a day, you tell Rick on *General Hospital* that the baby isn't his. You also tell your dog that the baby isn't Rick's. Your dog disagrees. You say to your dog, "Want to go outside now, stupid?" So your dog goes outside, and then immediately barks to come inside—and you are secretly relieved because this gives you something to do.

Being older involves inevitable "bootless nostalgia"—a morbid fascination with magazine articles entitled things like "Where Are They Now?" (In fact, one of the most difficult things about being a "celebrity" is the dread of seeing your photograph someday featured prominently in such an article. "Where Am I Now?" "*I* don't know," you say. "Where was I to begin with?" And then you realize you are talking to yourself.)

Nostalgia is probably one of the least cost-effective hobbies Americans can indulge in these days. Nine out of ten Americans (even *young* Americans) who try to go back to their ancestral family homes find that said domiciles have become a Pizza Hut. So that not only can you not go home again, you can forget about getting anchovies.

Which means that your only alternative is to think about the future.

There are probably two kinds of people in the world: those who care what happens after they pass on, and those who believe the ancient Sinhalese words "Bisreha singhe, muserwerwe ib unhh," which means roughly "Please keep the chewing-gum wrappers on my final square of earth to a minimum. And keep the noise down, too, okay? Guess that's all, now. Goodbye."

But most of us will confess to at least a passing interest in Larger Issues—when we hear the lone whistle of a freight train echoing late at night, or when the Voice of Your Announcer awakens you in the middle of your doze to say, "THIS IS A TEST. THIS IS ONLY A TEST . . ."

True Spirituality Revealed: The Short Form

A lot of people in modern life hear the word "religion" and look nervously at their shoes and hope someone will say, "Gee, I'd love to have your delicious Polynesian meatball recipe" before the conversation gets too freighted-with-import to handle.

Of course, we all wonder if God really exists, and more important, whether He remembers *we* exist. . . .

(And how is it that God can't find us, but JOE C. SPEDNICK, INCUMBENT DEMOCRAT RUNNING FOR STATE ASSEMBLY always can—and accordingly desires to send us unsolicited pictures of himself seated at his fake-mahogany desk and taking relaxing Sunday strolls with his overdressed family of five?)

People do sometimes wake up and get a little curious about questions like "Is life really just a foul, stinking morass of debts and blight and emptiness; a yawning void of shrieking, wintry oblivion; or will I probably feel better after another cup of coffee?"

We cannot even say anymore that "religion is the opiate of the masses," since *television* has become the new "opiate of the masses," and now television itself is being replaced by a generation of serious drug dependency, so that *opium* has finally become the "opiate of the masses," and "religion" is more out in the cold than ever before.

Not only have "churches" become "discos" where people with the morals of tarantulas dance the night away with white powder cascading from their nostrils, but the most common public outcry against these places is that on weekends, you have to know someone to get in.

No one can deny that we are experiencing a spiritual crisis in America unlike any before.

WHERE HAS THIS CRISIS ISSUED FROM?

For one thing, far too many of us number among the ranks of practicing *"Protestants."* Faced with the most theatrical sorts of religious fanaticism all over the world, American Protestants are forced to admit that they are adherents of THE WORLD'S MOST BORING RELIGION.

Protestants are a besieged race—herded into pachysandra ghettos, walled in by tasteful aluminum siding, besotted on low-salt potato chips, forced to get salon permanents so that our hair will attain more exciting contours. Traditional Protestantism has never known the joy of ritualized excess; it keeps its dogmas on a leash. Rather than bowing to an all-encompassing, eternal body of wisdom, it is the only religion that breaks down into *denominations.* (Scientists believe this is because *money* comes in "denominations.")

Protestants feel tragedy like everybody else, but nobody who wears putty-colored J. C. Penney slacks is very good at "singing the blues." We throw our heads back and our little pink mousy eyes water, and we say, "Euuuu, Lordy, I feel, like, so extremely low. . . ." And then we forget the rest of the words, and go out to buy some lawn food.

Most orthodox Protestants worship God and golfing attire, in that order, so that no one ever has to sacrifice an entire Sunday nailed to a pew; not when there are green, par-4 Elysian fields beckoning, and a few great damn drinks in the clubhouse afterwards.

But Protestants, and indeed Americans of all religious stripes, have important questions about spiritual existence, and yet we don't really know whom to ask, or how to phrase the questions without appearing obtuse, morally stunted, or worse.

But there are PROFESSIONAL SPIRITUAL ANSWER MEN who can address themselves to these questions, provided you agree to ask them anonymously. Here are the queries which come to light most often:

Q. Does God have a sense of humor?

A. He certainly does; but it isn't really like yours or my sense of humor. The United States Football League, the Nuclear Regulatory Commission, and the career of Lorenzo Lamas are all examples of God's sense of humor. God never really intended man to be able to laugh at His jokes. It never crossed His mind that we would "get" them, anyway.

Q. Does "the soul" exist?

A. Almost every religion that ever existed believes in some kind of vital "animus" inhabiting all living beings.

Natives of Papua New Guinea believe that "the soul" can be stolen by tourists' cameras, and before you think this is a foolish belief, think of all the people around you who have "no soul."

Think of your Aunt Yvonne, who still calls you Little Bethy and buys you wallets with little flamingoes on them, even though you are thirty-seven years old and a managing V.P. at E. F. Hutton. *This behavior is not her fault.* Her soul was stolen by a Brownie box camera in 1958 at a Memorial Day picnic, and so she has been forced to conduct herself very much like a *complete spazz* ever since. This is nothing to laugh about.

Q. Does this have anything to do with "good" and "bad" "KARMA"?

A. Okay, now we are getting to Eastern religions, so things are going to get considerably more complicated.

"KARMA" is a very important concept for everyone to understand, because even if you don't think you believe in it, it is a good idea to *start* believing immediately.

"Karma" was invented by Indian mystics in 600 B.C., and additionally by Beatle George Harrison in 1967, and has basically to do with *other lifetimes you don't know anything about.*

Let's say you used to be an unusually vicious pit bull in a previous life; and even though you are a saintly nun in this particular life, who gives to the poor on every possible occasion, *you will frequently lose your car keys* as a punishment for all the snarling and biting you did in your past life.

Sometimes "karma" affects you all in the same lifetime. It can be triggered by an attack of guilt or morbidness at any given point. If you break up with your girlfriend and tell her a lie to "spare her feelings" ("I can't have a relationship this month. I have jury duty"), THE SAME LIE WILL BE TOLD TO YOU WITHIN THE NEXT SIX MONTHS. AND YOU WILL RECOGNIZE IT.

Q. Is Buddhism something I CAN TRY IN THE PRIVACY OF MY OWN HOME?

A. Buddhism is probably the *best* religion for today's young, active professionals, but it will perhaps take a while to catch on, since it means renouncing *all your material possessions* (except for your umbrella and your rubber sandals, so you can at least go to the beach sometimes). But think of how many more material possessions you have now to renounce than you did twenty years ago (or for that matter, compared with the neighbors next door). That thought alone should fill you with a sort of hushed religious ecstasy.

Q. What's this I read about the never-ending struggle between "good" and "evil," "virtue" and "sin"?

A. You don't have to go any further than Great World Literature to know that this selfsame struggle has always been with us. Or just flip on your television set after 10 o'clock for the Duality of Mankind Hour, every Thursday and Friday, and Wednesday night. There are usually a number of women with very-blond or very-brunette hair; and exactly half of them are virtuous and half of them are Extremely Evil. (The brunette women are usually the evil ones, although they sometimes *disguise* themselves as the blond women in order to perform Weekly Acts of Assorted Wickedness.)

About ten minutes into the show, the women with the blond hair begin to cry. They usually say, "Oh,

Ray, I didn't mean for it to happen like this," or words to this effect. Usually, at some point in the show, the men named "Ray" get into a car in which Somebody Evil has tampered with the brakes, and then there is a very scary scene where "Ray" feels a need to drive along the coastline of Big Sur, very close to the edge, while he attempts to test his brakes. Meanwhile, back at the family homestead, one of the blond women is saying to the brunette woman that she feels a way with "Ray" that No Man Has Ever Made Her Feel Before, and later you see the dark-haired woman giving money to the man in the dark glasses who tampered with "Ray's" brakes.

If you watch the show a week later, you will get to see "Ray's" funeral.

The evil people usually do get punished in literature and on television, but not in any way that visibly affects the caliber of their wardrobe, or their interior decoration.

Q. If we are really fighting such a never-ending battle with the Forces of Darkness, then is there any merit to the phrase "Hell on Earth"? Or for that matter, "Heaven on Earth"?

A. People who have sinned more than once (which includes, more or less, everyone who has ever lived) report a common experience which goes something like this:

They have just walked into a sort of waiting hall, which looks exactly like Miami International Airport, and their flight from Houston was delayed for six hours because a wild bat flew into the cockpit, and now they are going to fetch their luggage. They watch the carousel spin—they count seventeen American Tourister suitcases similar to their own, only they all say "Raoul Lopez" on the tag. They wait until the carousel stops spinning, and a large crowd gathers, all of them *sans* luggage, wondering whether the carousel will ever spin again. "I *knew* I shouldn't have checked the plaid carry-on," sobs one woman. . . .

What these people are inexorably beginning to discover, of course, is that they have entered THE BAGGAGE RETRIEVAL OF THE DAMNED.

Yes, "Hell on Earth" takes many forms. Sometimes it takes the form of driving through a barren landscape where every single bar and restaurant says "REST ROOM FOR PATRONS ONLY," and there are cocktail waitresses with bazookas standing in every doorway. (Yes, there are "Rest Rooms of the Damned"! And there are also "Bridal Showers of the Damned"! There you are sitting in your lovely new living room, opening all your wedding presents and realizing 115 people have all given you sterling silver nut dishes shaped like puffins, and you are going to *have to send original thank-you notes for all of them.*)

There is no such thing as "Heaven on Earth," however. Most of us will never get up to Heaven, even if we are on the Frequent Flyer Plan. (And most of us are headed the other way, on the Frequent Fryer Program.)

Q. Is there such a thing, in the grand analysis, as the "afterlife"?

A. You know, this is what the whole problem is—a lot of us confuse the afterlife with "life after death," or reincarnation.

Reincarnation is sort of like this: Think about all those times you didn't want to eat your vegetables, and your father said, *"If you eat all your vegetables you will get a wonderful reward."* And you said, "What's the reward, Dad?" and he said, "A second helping."

The afterlife is a whole new menu.

THE AFTERLIFE, NOW REVEALED

We owe a great debt to people who journeyed right to the edge of the "other side" and came back to tell us all about it. Almost without exception, they reported it as being a supremely *peaceful* experience—beatific, floating; often there have been reunions with loved ones and family pets and sumptuous meals that lasted for hours and days at a time. Some have described the sensation of "standing on the shore of a river, waiting for a ferry to take me across." (Maybe this is hard to picture, but it's sort of like the summer ferry from Hyannis to Martha's Vineyard, only the passengers are of all races and religions, and they take you the minute you show up.) Once on the other side, the "ferryman" gently asks for a token fare payment, either in cash or by personal check (the ferryman has had to crack down lately on those who would use the eternally expired "Three Pieces of I.D. of the Damned").

If you are lucky enough to make it to "Heaven," it is because of either a lifetime of good deeds or a bookkeeping error. Only you will know the difference.

Heaven is a pretty wonderful place. Everyone lives in a lovely Colonial or Tudor-style home and has picnics for every meal. All the single women in Heaven are thin, wealthy professional vocalists. They either sing together in choirs, or tour Heaven individually as sold-out solo niteclub acts. Everyone has time to read a good book at night. All the teenagers in Heaven speak in complete sentences; all the pets in Heaven are self-cleaning, all the drinks are doubles, and all the men are President.

There isn't, actually, a lot to *do* in Heaven, but the thing is that Heaven is supposed to be "perfect." Not "interesting."

Heaven has been unlisted for a number of years now because a lot of the wrong people have been trying to talk themselves in.

Actually, they have some *very* attractive deals on "Purgatory," but some people just say, "Forget it. It's a comedown."

DOWN, PLEASE

A lot has been said about the eternal, writhing fires of damnation, most of it negative. And indeed, although you may have felt that life was a bit half-baked, you will find that "Hell" is always completely overcooked.

When you first arrive in Hell, you'll find a lot of people buried in muck with their feet sticking out. And there will be a lot of other people standing and holding cocktails, only trapped in a corner by people they will *never possibly have any interest in talking to, for any reason.*

Your former orthodontist is now residing in Hell, and still keeping office hours. All his appointments last eight years, and they never let you spit. All the girlfriends who broke up with you in high school are in Hell, but when you go up and say, "Cindy! Remember me?" they just fix their hair and ignore you. They're all engaged to the orthodontists, and they're busy every Saturday for the rest of eternity. The only places you can go in Hell to cool off are the movie theaters (the film industry is, of course, well represented in Hell), but they are always over–air-conditioned, so everyone usually walks out. At the Downtown Hell Triplex, they are showing *Heaven's Gate* for the next 6 million years, and all the people who financed the movie are strapped to their seats for all eternity.

Meanwhile, Back on Earth

THE majority of us who have any sense are generally happy that we won't be around to see what life on earth will be like in the future. Years and years before "1984" ever happened, George Orwell predicted that it would turn out to be *the year immediately following "1983"*—as well as a year full of paranoia, technical autocracy, and greed. Unfortunately, he was correct, and he was probably grateful that he never lived to see it happen. (In fact, how many times have you heard a person watching the 6 O'Clock News say, "Boy, I hoped I would never live to see *this*. . . ." The people you hear expressing this hope are turning out to be *younger* and *younger* every year. Either the world is changing faster and faster, or people are fine-tuning their disillusionment levels to a more and more sophisticated degree.)

A SHORT HISTORY OF PREDICTING THE FUTURE

For decades most American "hard" scientists pooh-poohed the existence of psychic phenomena and prescient thought, and for decades, most American PROFESSIONAL PSYCHICS were forced to make their predictions in the checkout line at supermarkets.

In Russia at least there are respected institutes of psychic phenomena, where prophetic, oracular dreams are analyzed, filed, and even subsidized by the Soviet Government. Soviet psychics knew years ago that Ursula Andress would bear one man's love child; and that this same man would later marry a lissome blond beauty from CBS's *Falcon Crest,* and that Miss Andress would still later bless the union in a poignant letter mailed from Gstaad, where Miss Andress was currently "in seclusion." This is why the Soviets are light-years ahead in ballistic and molecular technology. Not to mention that Soviet scientists can make Ping-Pong balls hang in midair through sheer force of psychic will, and that they can GUESS THE COLOR BLINDFOLDED OF RECTANGULAR SHEETS OF PAPER THAT THEY HAVE NEVER SEEN BEFORE.

Predicting the future has finally become an accredited science in America. (Which means that you can go to college and study "Futurology," become a "Futurist"; or else cut the class, or even show up for class five minutes later every day. "Futurology," by definition, *meets* five minutes later every day, because according to Einstein's law, if it met in the present, there would be two of everybody in the classroom. Something like that.)

People who can predict the future are becoming more prized and feared than ever before. Recently when a respected full-color newspaper held its annual "guest psychic" contest, a woman was given a cash reward for predicting "Increased tensions between the United States and the Soviet Union in the coming decade." No, this is not the sort of thing to be left to amateurs and housewives.

NOW, ON TO THE FUTURE

The following is a breakdown of probable future events in six major areas.

Politics, International and Domestic

- Psychics predict that in the future, supplies of petroleum, both domestic and Middle Eastern, will dwindle; as well as supplies of arable soil, potable water, and noncontaminated oxygen; and terrifyingly enough, there could be a MASSIVE SHORTAGE OF PHOTOGRAPHS OF PRINCESS DIANA.

While the world reels in shock, Middle Eastern terrorists will reveal that they are holding all existing negatives of photographs of the British princess until *People* magazine and *Redbook* agree to cough up $8 million. Purchasers of *People, McCall's, Redbook,* and others will have to settle for police sketches of Di, or photographs of lesser princesses, until the crisis can be averted.

Princess Anne will volunteer to release photographs of herself, but no one will honor her offer.

In a related crisis, Princess Diana will have a major falling-out with Prince Charles, briefly become engaged to singer Jimmy Page of Led Zeppelin, and come back to the Palace a week later in contrition and fatigue.

- In American politics, there will be a number of large-scale scandals involving bribes, kickbacks, and break-ins; and many Americans on television will profess great shock at hearing of "such high levels of corruption in government." These same citizens will also profess shock at finding "raisins" in "Raisin Bran," "holes" in doughnuts, and Former President Ulysses S. Grant actually buried in "Grant's Tomb."
- In the "Is Nothing Sacred?" category, the world will reel at the surprise revelation that THE "INTERNATIONAL DATE LINE" IS, IN FACT, A HOAX.

  Thousands of people in Tokyo and Manila will tearfully admit that they have been Scotch Taping tomorrow's date on their newspapers for years, just to show off and feel "more important" than Westerners. Ninety-six-year-old Former President Ronald Reagan will say, "Once again, a victory for good old-fashioned down-home Western supremacy that I guess kinda brings a lump to my throat."

Language and Communication

- In a related development, the U.S. Government will finally declare the existence of all languages other than English to be a hoax.

- The English language itself, however, will finally acknowledge a revolution that has been going on for decades. There is a high potential that by the year 2000, the letter *'N'* will be accepted as a serious word in the English lexicon (as in "Day 'n' Night," "Sturm 'n' Drang," and "Health 'n' Human Services")—this despite protests by linguists and grammarians who will camp out on the Capitol steps, too late to stop a joint resolution by the Senate 'n' the House of Representatives.
- All future communications will be speeded up to an even more frightening degree than heretofore experienced. Overnight courier services will multiply. They will actually find a way to make Priority Parcels travel faster than the speed of light. ("Relativity Express—for When It Absolutely, Positively Has to Be There Yesterday.")
- In a move reflective of Americans' increasingly "Born to Weekend" lifestyle, the new 1988 grammar textbooks will commence with the controversial verb conjugation "TO ANTIQUE": "I ANTIQUE," "WE ANTIQUE," "I MIGHT HAVE ANTIQUED," "WE SHOULD HAVE ANTIQUED," "GEOFF AND BEVERLY ALL-TOO-FREQUENTLY ANTIQUED," and so on.
- There will be an increasing controversy over the effect of long-term television-watching among the youth of America. Stuntman Evel Knievel will attempt to leap across the brain synapses of a teenage boy who has been watching MTV almost continuously since the age of five; but he will be unable to find any reputable underwriters willing to insure the stunt.

Entertainment and the Media

- In keeping with the "Guess Again—I Am Not a Bimbo" movement, former *Dallas* star Charlene Tilton late in 1989 will decide that she wants to "not just act, but direct." Her first, much-lauded effort will be a *CBS Sunday Night Movie* about the long-suppressed problem of organized cannibalism in America's suburbs. The movie will star Cheryl Ladd, Robert Urich, Conrad Bain, and exciting newcomer Dweezil Zappa. (The working title "Eat Your Heart Out" will be changed to "Springtime for June and Dick Mackenzie.")

- Commercial movie distributors will continue to experience enormous setbacks, as patrons persist in renting movies on videotape and playing them at home on their VCRs.

  A lot of people, though, will experience a growing nostalgia for the "total movie experience"—the way they remember it from their long-ago childhoods. So the "Total Movie Experience" will soon be available in the *home.* If you supply the Paul Newman Movietime Popcorn, you will be able to hire "ushers" to show you to your couch, and for a small surcharge, you can have a fat girl sit behind you and snap her gum throughout the entire movie, or she can bring along a friend and explain the movie to the friend in a very loud voice, only she will get all the important details completely wrong, and you can turn around and tell her to shut up, and she can say, "Go to hell," and then you can hire a neighbor to stand by your door in a loud sports jacket and tell you you cannot have a refund, and he's sorry you've had a terrible evening, but it isn't his fault.
- Fitness superstar *Jane Fonda* will finally admit to massive fraud on her best-selling exercise video *Jane Fonda's* New *Advanced Workout for the 1990s.* (You know how at the end of the video, Jane clasps her hands, looks deeply into your eyes, and says, "You did a *great job*"? She lied.)
- In the year 1994, the entire entertainment industry will be rocked by the naked admission in *Variety* and *Billboard* that "THERE WILL NEVER BE ANY NEW IDEAS FOR MOVIES, OR ANYTHING ELSE, UNTIL THE END OF TIME."

Love 'n' Dating

- Even now, in the present day, dating life is dangerously perverse, since it is highly acceptable for a fourteen-year-old girl to call an eleven-year-old boy and ask him for a date—and it is highly probable that he will say

"Not tonight" because he has to wash his hair. And he will be telling the truth.

Romance in the nineties will increasingly be seen as a hindrance to what's *really* important (i.e., making more money than anyone who has ever lived in the entire world). Many women will have an actual fear of meeting Mr. Right, as they will no longer have any excuse to stay until 9:30 at the office and gnaw their bleeding cuticles.

A new service springing up will be DATING SERVICES FOR THE ADMITTEDLY AND UNABASHEDLY SUPERFICIAL.

Presently, many single people run ads in various "personal columns" describing and cataloguing their numerous sensitive qualities: love of animals, fondness for tender snowfalls and charming antiques, and so forth and so on. In the nineties, everyone will simply get tired of lying and will be glad to abandon the pretense once and for all.

The entire notion of "Mr. Right" will be replaced by "Mr. That's Completely Correct"—a man who has your same exact values (he loves money very, very much, and hopes someday to be buried with it). He drives a Meaningful Car, and went to college in one of the Original Thirteen Colonies (although there will be some desperate types around who will swear that someone from Arizona once signed the Bill of Rights). Formal courtship will make a profound comeback—there will be a massive rash of people being Seriously Engaged to Discuss a Potential Wedding; after which people will report being Swept Away on a Tide of Cautious Optimism.

Very meaningful and profitable experiences will be had by all.

Fashion

- The science of fashion and appearance will become more important to Americans than ever before. In fact, a number of people under intensive psychiatric treatment, previously considered completely unequipped to function in normal society, will be miraculously cured overnight by "having their color swatches done."
- The location of the "fashion capital of the world" will continue to be hotly argued over by fashion arbiters

around the globe. A number of arbiters will threaten suicide when, in a surprise, tie-breaking ballot, the "fashion capital of the world" is declared to be "Seattle, Washington."

Medicine

- In the future, much more research will be done on the subject of "good stress." "Not all stress is harmful or undesirable," say leading scientists in our fast-paced, go-getter world; and in the future we can expect to see much more research on "good" anxiety; "good" hypertension; "good" attempted wrist-slashing; and "good" crippling chest pains.
- In the late 1990s, a number of psychiatric patients will try to overturn the assertion by mental-health professionals around the world that "Money Does Not Buy Happiness."

  Many of these desperate individuals will be secretly filmed south of the American border buying "Happiness" in cheap Tijuana establishments, and trying to smuggle it on their persons back into the United States. Apprehended by U.S. border officials, they will insist that they were only bringing the "Happiness" back "for friends," and that they were not intending to sell or profit from it in any way.

  The FDA will insist that further testing will need to be done before "Happiness" or any like substance will be made available to U.S. nationals on an over-the-counter basis.
- Finally, fans of Elvis Presley will be happy to hear that *cloning* work is being done on the entertainer around the clock, using clippings of the singer's hair and fingernails as well as the signatures and carbons from his MasterCard receipts.

  A snag will develop when people realize that ELVIS almost always handed over responsibility for his personal finances to his business manager, so the future result may well be an all-singing, all-dancing COLONEL TOM PARKER.

Epilogue

Let's Get Metaphysical

If you ever believed you could keep life from being a "disillusioning experience," you must have been listening to Jiminy Cricket when he sang that little song in *Pinocchio* about "Wishing on a Star." (If you want to listen to the philosophies of animated-cartoon insects in tiny spats and three-piece suits, this is not very much to your credit, but it is also nothing at all to be *embarrassed* about.)

So many of the negative conclusions we've drawn about life are erroneous, foolish and exaggerated. It is probably not true, for example, that the whole world is out to get you at any given time. (At any given time, only about 20 percent of the world is out to get you. The rest of the world has your mailing address, just in case.)

But maybe you have been wandering around and thinking, "There has got to be some kind of level of meaning which exists in *other* people's lives, which has somehow never revealed itself to me. I see it on their faces; I know that something is there, but I just cannot put my finger on it."

Okay, you aren't really going to like this, but you know that week you had the flu back in fourth grade, and you came back and everyone in school seemed "different" to you? That week your entire class was taken to see an Indian Mystic, and he completely explained the Whole Shebang to them, and afterwards, they got to have ice cream.

THE TRUE SECRET OF HAPPINESS

Life lets you down sometimes, admittedly, because *nothing is ever as good as the first time* (and after a while, you run out of things that you have never, consciously, done before).

Your first kiss; your first prom; the first time you land your "Q" on a "triple word score" in *Scrabble,* and your grandmother accused you of cheating. (She is so very proud that you've figured out how she's been cheating for the last forty years. Your grandfather never figured it out.)

HAPPINESS IS SOMETHING THAT STRIKES YOU BY *ACCIDENT,* LIKE A BOLT OF LIGHTNING, OR A CHANCE AVALANCHE, OR A TRUCK WITHOUT BRAKES ON A 40-PERCENT-GRADE HIGHWAY. It doesn't always strike the *right* people. (It has always struck DOLLY PARTON, who seems to deserve it, and LEO BUSCAGLIA, who probably does not.)

A lot of people express the fear "What if I reach a phase of complete bliss and contentment in my life, and *don't even know it*?" And indeed, it is highly possible to miss the signs, or notice them only when it is too late. It could happen at the moment the gas-station attendant is saying, "Regular or Unleaded?" and by the time you pull out your Sunoco card, it is already too late.

People think that happiness means winning a million dollars, or being friends with someone who has a million dollars, or having children who are Miss America, or whatever—

BUT HAPPINESS MEANS, BY SIMPLE DEFINITION, THAT YOU SIMPLY AVERTED ALL THE TERRIBLE THINGS THAT COULD HAPPEN TO YOU ON ANY GIVEN DAY.

You know the feeling: when you thought you probably lost your checkbook on the bus, but then it shows up in the backseat of your car, or in the little crack next to your refrigerator, and you say, "That's pretty good. I did not lose my checkbook AFTER ALL." If you manage not to lose your checkbook for several decades at once, YOU COULD TURN OUT TO BE ONE OF THE HAPPIEST PEOPLE ON EARTH.

Think of all the people in Bangladesh and Pakistan who never worry about losing their checkbooks, and if you are very, very lucky, you can be like them.

Every year, the chaos and randomness and stress of life affect millions of people, so that they shout out the words "I am being *driven to distraction*!" But most of them never truly arrive there, usually due to traffic.

Always remember that there is *no need to panic,* and above all THAT WE HAVE NOTHING TO FEAR—but Life Itself.

ACKNOWLEDGMENTS

Without the help of the following, I never would have made it through *Life* alive: Lilian Eng, Josie Ferrara, Jenny and Meredith Brush, Nancy Hart and Judy McCann, and the ever-agreeable Val and Kevin Weaver. I am especially grateful to Heidi Chase and Eileen Brideau for laughing when it was crucial.

Most importantly, I owe a great debt to Marjorie Williams for editing the uneditable and fathoming the unfathomable; to Patricia Brush for her valuable labor in 1954 and 1986; to Bob for being my second brain; to my publisher, Joni Evans, for being the first to warn me; and to Richard Pine for working harder than anyone I know for 15 percent.

ABOUT THE AUTHOR

Stephanie Brush is the author of *Men: An Owner's Manual.* She was born in Cleveland, Ohio, and grew up in Pleasantville, New York. She has written for numerous publications, including *Cosmopolitan, People, Self, Vogue, Signature, Family Weekly,* and *Mademoiselle,* and now lives in southern Connecticut. The greatest moment of her life was the day when she turned up as an "answer" in the *New York Times* Sunday Acrostic Puzzle.